RIVER
of Fire,
RIVER
of Water

An Introduction
to the
Pure Land
Tradition of
Shin Buddhism

DOUBLEDAY

New York   London
Toronto   Sydney   Auckland

RIVER
of Fire,
RIVER
of Water

TAITETSU
UNNO

南無阿彌陀佛

PUBLISHED BY DOUBLEDAY
a division of Bantam Doubleday Dell
Publishing Group, Inc.
1540 Broadway, New York, New York 10036

DOUBLEDAY and the portrayal of an anchor with a
dolphin are trademarks of Doubleday, a division of
Bantam Doubleday Dell Publishing Group, Inc.

BOOK DESIGN BY DONNA SINISGALLI

Library of Congress Cataloging-in-Publication Data
Unno, Taitetsu, 1929–
River of fire, river of water : an introduction to the
Pure Land tradition of Shin Buddhism / by Taitetsu
Unno.
      p.   cm.
   1. Shin (Sect)—Doctrines—Introductions.   2. Pure
Land Buddhism—Doctrines—Introductions.   I. Title.
         BQ8718.5.U66   1998
      294.3'926—dc21   97-45499
                              CIP
         ISBN 978-0-385-48511-1

147514730

To
my father
who taught me to see
what eyes cannot see

A Note from the Author

The calligraphy on the book cover is from *Tannisho* II: "Since I am absolutely incapable of any religious practice . . . (*izure no gyo myo oyobi gataki mi nareba . . .*)." The calligraphy used throughout the book at the start of each section is the Name, "namu-amida-butsu."

ACKNOWLEDGMENTS

The idea for this little book came from Trace Murphy, editor at
Doubleday, who felt a strong need for the aspect of compassion
in Buddhism to be more widely introduced to the general public.
He thus invited me to write on Pure Land Buddhism for the
interested reader who has had some acquaintance with the other
better-known forms of Buddhism, such as Zen, Tibetan, and
Vipassana. In order to meet his request I have kept the tone
nonacademic and incorporated personal anecdotes, stories, and
poetry from various sources. I wish to thank Trace for the opportunity to undertake this project, which is a new venture for
me, but I am delighted to share with the reader my understanding of compassion-in-action, the singular characteristic permeating the great Buddhist tradition.

It is impossible to mention all the people, both known and
unknown, who have contributed to the making of this book, but
I wish to thank three parties that gave me encouragement
throughout the process. They include the members of the Shin
Buddhist Sangha of Northampton, who read several versions of
River of Fire, River of Water; my friends and colleagues across the

country—Alfred Bloom, Ruth Tabrah, Kenneth Tanaka, Alexander Eliot, Dennis Hudson, Abram Yoshida, Ty-Ranne Grimstad, my little bodhisattva Shaypa; and my wife and partner Alice, who is also my best critic, for her perceptive reading and insightful suggestions. To them all, I give infinite thanks.

CONTENTS

PREFACE

Whether teaching Asian religions at Smith College or appearing at international conferences on religious studies, Professor Unno always strives to inculcate deep hearing and soul-tact. Self-contained, self-effacing, and dryly humorous, he turns the ongoing "dialogue" between Eastern and Western cultures into friendly, fruitful conversation.

While D. T. Suzuki was the first to open American minds to Zen Buddhism, now with this book Unno brilliantly introduces a different, far more popular Buddhist faith; namely, the ancient Pure Land tradition as developed by Honen and Shinran in thirteenth-century Japan. This dynamic and important religion is something that few Westerners ever heard of—until now.

The genius of Honen and Shinran, Unno tells us, was that they "discovered the way to bring Buddhist truth alive in the midst of the householder's life. . . . In the words of Shinran,

> All people—men, women high or low station—
> In saying the Name of Amida are not restricted

To walking, standing, sitting, or reclining,
Nor to time, place, or conditions."

What else distinguishes this popular faith from elitist Zen?
Unno responds with a wonderfully concise quote from Honen:
"In the Path of Sages one perfects wisdom and achieves enlightenment; in the Path of Pure Land one returns to the foolish self
to be saved by Amida."

But return "to the foolish self" is no easy matter. On that
path, too, struggle and suffering ensue. "Alienation," the modern bugaboo, is nothing new. Witness Homer's Achilles, Shakespeare's Hamlet, and Kafka's relatively blameless "K." The pro-
tagonist in Dante's *Divine Comedy* may have hoped to go straight
up, but found he had to go down first. And so it is with all of
us.

Unno states the case bluntly: "The question becomes deeply
personal and existential. Who am I? Where did my life come
from? Where is it going? What is the purpose of my life? How
do I cope with death and dying? In trying to fathom the answers
we struggle to contend with oneself, with one's own darkness,
with one's self-delusions."

Yet there is no preaching here. Instead, Unno gives us poi-
gnant stories, occasionally hilarious personal anecdotes, and
plain but lovely translations from appropriate texts. Consider for
example Basho's justly famous haiku:

Such stillness—
The cry of the cicadas
Sinks into the rocks.

This poem, Unno says, "points to a happening taking place at
the deepest level of life, unifying the cry, the rocks, the poet, and

the universe into a singular experience." Taking his courage in his hands and with Basho's inspiration full upon him, Umio thereupon appends a profoundly insightful haiku of his own:

> Such sorrow—
> The cry of true compassion
> Sinks into my hard ego.

One is forcibly reminded of these lines from Euripides' *Helen* in J. T. Sheppard's translation:

> I had washed my robes of red
> And on fresh green rushes spread
> In the meadows by the cool
> Darkly gleaming waterpool
> For the golden sun to dry,
> When I heard a voice, a cry;
> such a cry as ill would suit
> the happy music of my lute:
> And I wondered what might be
> the cause of that strange minstrelsy,
> so sad, and yet so wondrous clear.

Some Bible verses return as well:

> A voice said "Cry!"
> and I said, "What shall I cry?"
> "All flesh is grass"?
>
> Surely the People is grass.

Rudolph Steiner's lecture *On Evil* (given in Berlin during the dark winter of the First World War) argued that "The root of all evil in human nature is what we call egoism. Every kind of human imperfection, of evil from insignificant shortcomings to the worst crimes, can be traced to this single trait." And yet, Steiner went on to assert, an alert sense of self is required for spiritual development: "When we enter the spiritual world, even if it is through the portal of death, we must live with the strength which we have developed in our inner being. But we cannot acquire this strength there; it must have been gained by living an altruistic life in the physical world."

We are indeed as blades of grass or flowers in the meadow. To unfold, refine, rejoice, and fulfill one's personal self in this unrepeatable life seems a natural enough ideal. But human egoism remains a wellspring of evil! That's the terrible paradox, the living contradiction, which confronts each one of us from day to day. It makes the world go around, one might say, and there's nothing we can do to make the paradox go away. Yet religion, contemplation, art, and poetry, all four can help illuminate the further horizon of reality. As Shinran exults:

> When the many rivers of evil passion enter
> Into the ocean of the Great Compassionate Vow
> Of Unhindered Light, illuminating the ten quarters,
> They become one in taste with the water of wisdom.

Yes, East and West do meet. They always have. For we are all one people, an ignorant and self-destructive lot—yet simultaneously blessed to be alive.

> The heavens declare the glory of God
> And the firmament showeth his handiwork

Day unto day utttereth speech
And night unto night showeth knowledge.

It's not so much to say that Unno bares the heart of Shin
Buddhism. Like Quaker Christianity, for instance, his religion is
not intellectual but contemplative, not hierarchical but egalitar-
ian. His exposition of his faith remains intellectual by necessity,
yet poetic as well. Indeed it runs bubbly-clear, like a trout
stream; the trout being his own humble heart. Hence for this
reader at least, Unno's book goes well beyond its stated aim. It
has improved my understanding of my own faith—and even of
myself.

ALEXANDER ELIOT
VENICE, 1997

PROLOGUE

There are eighty-four thousand paths to liberation and freedom from self-delusion, according to Buddhism. This wealth of possibilities may seem to make liberation more than accessible, but they are not spelled out in some enlightenment mail-order catalog. Which path a person takes is often not a matter of choice but decided by the accidents of birth, circumstance, encounters, and quirks of fate. Yet there are defining moments for each of us that can change the entire course of life. Such a moment for me was the shocking suicide of my best friend. I was twenty-four at that time.

I had been in Japan for two years, following my graduation from the University of California at Berkeley in 1951. My ambition was to become a Buddhist scholar. Through the intermediary of D. T. Suzuki, whom I had met during my senior year in San Francisco, I enrolled in the Tokyo University graduate school as a special student before matriculating in the regular program in Buddhist Studies.

Living in Japan, which at that time was still suffering the devastation of World War II, I came to have mixed feelings about my new home. Having grown up in a Japanese-American family, I could easily identify with its rich cultural past but not with its contemporary history and its people. It was difficult to fully comprehend the kind of suffering that war had brought to them. And yet, in America, I had never really felt at home either. My family and I had been among one hundred twenty-thousand Americans of Japanese ancestry who had been incarcerated behind barbed-wire fences in "concentration camps," (so-called by then President Franklin D. Roosevelt) without due process of law. Now in Japan but still lost and confused, a stranger in a strange land, I was searching for some kind of mooring. It was at that point that I was befriended by Teruo, a brilliant, older philosophy student also at Tokyo University.

I felt a close kinship with him, in part because of our shared interest in discussing issues of a philosophical nature. We compared notes on Japanese and American cultures, gossiped about professors we knew and about courses we took, exchanged notes on impetuous liaisons with the opposite sex, and shared our dreams and hopes for the future. But a dark, persistent cloud hovered over the bright promise of Teruo's future: his frail health, due to tuberculosis in his youth. Effective medical treatment was lacking at that time, and his body had been ravaged by the effects of the disease. He was frequently exhausted and in great pain. He became increasingly frustrated that he could not sustain the vigorous demands of a highly competitive academic life. One day of hard studying needed to be compensated by two full days of quiet rest.

When we experience pain and suffering, it is only natural to ask "Why?" Such was probably the case when Teruo one day asked me, "What is karma in Buddhism?" It was on the eve of his graduation from the university, and we were sitting having a beer in a German-speaking bar in Tokyo's Ginza district. I failed to appreciate the deep feeling that motivated his question, and I glibly quoted some abstract theories that I had just read in a Buddhist text and abruptly changed subjects. As we left the bar to go home, Teruo said that he had tickets for a dance the next evening. We said good night, and I promised him that I would drop by his home the following afternoon. We could go to the social together.

The following day, as promised, I went to his home shortly after the noon hour. When I knocked on the door, Teruo's mother came to the door with a worried look on her face. In an anxious whisper, she said, "Teruo didn't come home last night!" Knowing that he could have stayed out all night drinking (as he sometimes did) I calmly assured her, "I'm sure that he'll be home soon. I'll come back again later."

Late that afternoon I went to a noodle shop. The evening edition of the newspaper had just arrived, and as I picked up the paper, I read the headline with horror—"College Student Commits Suicide." I instantly knew that it was Teruo. He had taken an overdose of sleeping pills, swallowing them with soft drinks, in the compounds of a Zen monastery south of Tokyo. Did he decide to take his life because of his failing health, the anxiety of academic competition, or some unknown existential crisis?

I rushed back to his home, hoping somehow to comfort his mother, who had also just heard the tragic news of her son. Devastated, she had lost her only son upon whom she had showered love and affection, and she just wailed in grief and mourning. This went on and on. Though I searched desperately for words to express my sympathy and for words that might comfort her, none came forth.

That evening, I stayed up all night going over the tragic happening again and again. Three questions loomed large in my mind. First, I wondered if Teruo was now happy—was he now at peace? I thought about this for a long time, but instead of an answer coming to me there was only silence. Secondly, I wondered what I could say to Teruo's mother. What is the one word of compassion that I could offer her for her painful loss? I wasn't looking for hackneyed phrases of condolence but truly uplifting words. But again, I didn't know—there was only a void. And thirdly, I kept thinking of Teruo's question to me—what is karma, really? As I thought deeply about it, I realized that such an objective question, having little to do with my own existence, would invite only empty, abstract answers, answers of the sort I had given Teruo on the previous night. For a truly meaningful answer, the question of karma had to become more concrete: Who am I? What am I? Where did my life come from and where was it going? There was only a blank.

I thus found myself at an absolute impasse. I could not change the past. I could not go forward. I could not stay still and find peace in the present. Somehow I would have to find my way out of this predicament, but I felt truly lost. Yet, as all these questions and frustrations were circulating in my mind, I remembered the Pure Land parable of the two rivers and white path. Attributed to Shan-tao, the Pure Land master of seventh-century China, it captures the existential predicament in which one is made to awaken the aspiration for enlightenment (*bodhicitta*). My painful struggle became slowly illuminated by this ancient parable.

In the parable, a traveler is journeying through an unknown and dangerous wilderness. Soon he is pursued by bandits and wild beasts, and he races to get away from them. Running westward, he eventually comes to a river divided into two, separated by a narrow white path. The white path is only a few inches wide and runs from the near shore to the far shore. On one side of the path the river is filled with leaping flames that reach

Courtesy of the Kawasaki City Art Museum

twenty feet into the air; on the other, the deep river has a
powerful current that overflows with dangerous waves. Even
though the white path is the only possibility of escape across the
perilous river, it is not an alternative because of lapping fire and
waves. Filled with fear, the traveler cannot go forward, cannot go
back, and cannot stand still. In the words of Shan-tao, he faces
"three kinds of imminent death."

Just at that time, the desperate traveler hears a calming voice
right behind him on the eastern shore, urging him to go forward
on the white path: "Go forth without fear; no danger exists. But
if you remain, you will surely die!" Just then, he hears a beckoning call from the far shore: "Come just as you are with singleness
of heart. Do not fear the flames and waves; I shall protect you!"

Shan-tao tells us that the river of fire connotes anger; the
river of water, greed. The two joined together make an odd
picture, but they illustrate how the overflowing abundance of
greed and anger can fill our lives. In our greed we want to make
life move according to our desires. When we do not get our way,
our passions are stifled and anger erupts.

The eastern shore, the side where the traveler encountered
his dilemma, is the world of delusion—samsara. The western
shore is the Other Shore of enlightenment—nirvana. While this
side is the defiled land, the far side is known as the Pure Land.
Connecting the two is a narrow, white path. The tenuousness of
the path shows the weakness of human aspiration to break
through self-delusion into liberation and freedom.

The pursuing bandits represent enticing teachings that
abound in our world, all promising immediate material benefits
and psychological relief. They may provide temporary answers
but no true liberation. The wild beasts manifest instinctual passions that keep us bound to this shore of delusion. Both pull us
away from moving forward on the path. The voice of encourage-

ment from the eastern shore is that of the historical Buddha, the teachings of Sakyamuni; the beckoning call from the western shore comes from the Buddha of Immeasurable Light and Immeasurable Life, Amida. As one heeds the urging of Sakyamuni, the aspiration to move forward becomes pure and powerful. And as one embodies the call of Amida, it becomes single-minded and unshakable. This aspiration for supreme enlightenment is none other than the white path, now expanded and made safe, now an open passage through the flames of anger and waves of greed.

But even though the first step has been taken on the path, the threat is not over. As the traveler moves forward, the bandits make enticing promises and the beasts offer all kinds of temptations, attempting to call him back to this shore of delusion. But, sustained by the words of Sakyamuni and the call of Amida, the traveler does not hesitate, moves forward, and reaches the Other Shore safely into the waiting arms of a good friend (*kalyanamitra*) who is none other than Amida Buddha.

In reflecting on the parable I saw myself as that traveler, a sojourner in life with a checkered history. Pushed by false ambitions and pursued by demons within, I now confronted "three kinds of certain death." While being comforted to see my predicament described precisely by this parable, it did not tell me enough about how to get out of it. I began desperately searching for teachers to point the way. When I could not find anyone around me, I began a random, voracious reading of existential literature—Camus, Sartre, Nietzsche, Heidegger—and the scriptures of world religions—Buddhist literature, including contemporary intepretations, the Bhagavad Gita, Lao-tzu and Chuang-tzu, the New Testament, and so on. Some of this was useful on one level, but none cleared the confusion that prevailed. The glaring light of day was difficult to bear, the darkness of night seemed to lessen the agitation, alcohol definitely eased the pain. At one time I thought of abandoning my studies altogether; at another time I played with the idea of becoming a monk.

Slowly, however, after months of indecision and uncertainties, I began to find a faint sense of direction. The weight of my family background—generations of Shin Buddhist priests on both my mother's and father's sides—became decisive. Until that point my interest in Buddhism was primarily academic; in fact, I had little interest in the solace it promised, especially in its Pure Land form. But now my focus became a personal quest. As I moved forward on the white path, the world of Japanese Pure Land opened up. Welcomed by fine teachers and exemplary lay devotees, they helped me to formulate answers, however tentative, to the three questions that had arrested the course of my life. But the process of finding inner peace was not easy because of the maze of abstruse doctrines and technical religious terms that I needed to unravel. I needed to reduce them to the point that they resonated with the pragmatic turn in my nature. My varied excursions since that time into philosophical, religious, and psychological fields have focused on pursuing answers within the framework of the three basic questions concerning death and dying, the meaning of true compassion, and my karmic existence as infinite finitude.

As I proceeded on my quest, I discovered that these questions are not uncommon among contemporary people, regardless of religious affiliation or lack thereof. For who has not lost someone close because of cancer or the scourge of AIDS and not questioned the person's fate? Who has not sought the one word of compassion to share with those who experience irretrievable, painful loss? And who has not questioned oneself, as Tolstoy's Ivan Ilyich did, when he asked at the end of his seemingly successful career as a high court judge, "What if my entire life, my entire conscious life, was *not the real thing?*"

All world religions grapple with these questions, but in my case, due to fortunate karmic circumstances, Shin Buddhism provides the answers that are illuminating, challenging, and constantly evolving. Despite the wealth of possibilities we may seem to have in the eighty-four thousand paths to enlightenment, it is through encountering great difficulties and reaching an incredible impasse—as the traveler did—that we discover our individual paths. The Pure Land tradition has been my path. It is because of my own personal experience with it that I wish to share it with those who may not be too familiar with the depth, scope, and richness of this significant expression of Buddhism. To begin with we need to briefly trace the historical evolution of Pure Land Buddhism.

THE HISTORICAL
LEGACY

The beginnings of the Pure Land tradition go back to the time of the emergence of Mahayana Buddhism in the first century B.C.E., approximately five centuries after the founding of the religion by the historical Buddha in India. The Pure Land way bases its teaching on three Mahayana scriptures: *The Larger Sutra of Pure Land, The Smaller Sutra of Pure Land,* and *The Sutra on Contemplating Amida Buddha.* Known commonly today as the Triple Sutras, they originated in India and Central Asia and came to Japan in the sixth century soon after the introduction of Buddhism to this island nation. But during this early period few took notice of these writings. Even the monk-scholars who were the most literate people around regarded them as secondary.

A familiarity with these essential sutras helps us appreciate some of the unique aspects of Pure Land Buddhism. *The Larger Sutra,* also known as

the *Sutra of Immeasurable Life*, contains a discourse given by Sakyamuni Buddha at the Mount of Vulture Peak in Rajagriha, India. He tells the story of Dharmakara who makes a series of
forty-eight vows to save all beings, ultimately fulfills them, and
attains supreme enlightenment to become Amida Buddha—the
Buddha of Immeasurable Light and Life. This is a story that is
not a story but the emergence of fundamental reality in a person's life.

The *Smaller Sutra* is a much shorter scripture that depicts the
indescribable beauty of the Pure Land in fantastic imagery, symbolic of the state of supreme enlightenment. The *Sutra on Contemplating Amida* outlines sixteen forms of meditative practice that
leads to liberation and freedom.

Buddhism in Japan grew rapidly in the sixth century under
imperial and aristocratic patronage. It was welcomed as the car-
rier of continental civilization, inspiring art and architecture,
painting and sculpture, poetry and prose literature. It also enriched the people's lives by improving the quality of life—
founding clinics, orphanages, public bathhouses—and by pro-
moting learning—agriculture, bridge building, sericulture, medi-
cine, and astronomy. The great Mahayana schools of Sanron,
Kegon, and others, originating in India or China, became established by the Nara period (710–794); and the Tendai and Shingon schools flourished among imperial and aristocratic circles in
the Heian era (794–1185). During this time, the Pure Land
teachings and practices gradually became known among individual clerics and slowly spread among the populace.

The Buddhism for the elite, however, gradually declined in
power and influence with inevitable historical changes in the
eleventh and twelfth centuries. As the established social order
disintegrated, the Pure Land movement spread among all classes,

especially welcomed by those who had been excluded from the monastic path. The Primal Vow of Amida, the Buddha of Immeasurable Light and Life, now appeared as a major force on the stage of history.

In the year 1175 the Tendai monk Honen broke with the established center of monastic learning, Mt. Hiei, and proclaimed the establishment of an independent Jodo or Pure Land school. While Pure Land practices had been pursued within the established schools, it was always adjunct to some form of traditional religious disciplines. The contemplation on the virtues of Amida and the Pure Land, for example, was practiced among small groups of the upper classes, but it was never a separate, distinct path in itself. But with the founding of an independent Pure Land school, Honen rejected the meditative approach and advocated the singular practice of recitative nembutsu, the intoning of "namu-amida-butsu" (I entrust myself to Amida Buddha). This simple practice was the act selected by the Buddha for all people living in the age of *mappo*, the endtime of history. The endtime had arrived, as evident in the earthquakes, floods, drought, famine, pestilence, civil wars, and conflagrations that swept the capital and the countryside. As the world became increasingly unstable and chaotic, traditional Buddhism, supported by the privileged classes, became increasingly irrelevant to the times, and the demand for a new religiosity to meet the spiritual needs of the age became intense.

The void was filled by the newly established Pure Land teaching of recitative nembutsu. It met the spiritual hunger of the people and attracted a mass following. For those who had been excluded from the Buddhist path, it was the saving grace. Those who had been excluded were fishermen and hunters who made a living by violating the precept of noninjury, peasants who were considered "bad," lowly and ignorant, women of all classes because of their defilements, and monks and nuns who had broken the monastic precepts.

Among Honen's disciples was Shinran (1173–1263), a relatively unknown monk, who had left the Tendai monastery at Mt. Hiei and became his devoted disciple in 1201. Soon after, in the year 1207, accused of inciting social disturbance for preaching the Pure Land way, Honen and his disciples, including Shinran, were branded common criminals and exiled to remote provinces. The popular Pure Land movement had created a schism in society, and the lower classes, inflamed by religious fervor, denounced and desecrated the Buddhas other than Amida and the native deities. Honen admonished his followers against these excesses, but nevertheless he was held responsible.

Honen died in 1212 soon after his pardon in Kyoto, but Shinran remained in the outlying provinces to spread the nembutsu teaching. After several decades, he eventually returned to Kyoto and died in the year 1263. Thereupon, his descendants and followers established a separate school, called Jodo Shinshu, and regarded him as the founder. He himself had no such intention, for his aim was to simply expound "the true teaching (Shinshu) of Pure Land (Jodo)" as taught by his teacher Honen. Jodo Shinshu is also known as Shin Buddhism, and sometimes it is used synonymously with Pure Land Buddhism. This identification, however, is misleading because there are other forms of Pure Land teachings besides Shin Buddhism in Japan, Korea, China, and Vietnam.

Shinran based his teaching on the three Pure Land scriptures and claimed a lineage inspired by the Primal Vow of Amida Buddha and first articulated in the *Larger Sutra* by Sakyamuni Buddha. The Japanese Pure Land lineage was transmitted through history from India to China to Japan by seven masters:

Nagarjuna (c. 150–250) and Vasubandhu (fifth century) of India; T'an-luan (476–542), Tao-ch'o (562–645), and Shan-tao (613–687) of China; Genshin (942–1017) and Honen (1133–1212) of Japan.

The new school stood out in many ways from the traditions that preceded it, particularly in the way that it could be integrated into common, everyday life. Shin Buddhism makes no sharp distinction between clergy and laity as far as the possibility of enlightenment is concerned. Everyone, regardless of differences in age, class, gender, profession, or moral culpability, would attain Buddhahood by the working of great compassion. It naturally followed that this religious path would be harmonious with family life. Consequently, marriage was approved, and the time-honored celibacy of monastic life was reversed, beginning with Shinran himself, who got married and openly negated the time-honored monastic ideal of celibacy. The *dojo* or "training place" for the practice of Buddhism is everyday, secular life, not some cloistered enclosure or privileged space. That Honen and Shinran discovered the way to bring the Buddhist truth alive in the midst of the householder's life was real genius. In the words of Shinran:

> All people—men, women, high or low station—
> In saying the Name of Amida are not restricted
> To walking, standing, sitting, or reclining,
> Nor to time, place, or conditions.

THE COLOR GOLD

2

南無阿彌陀佛

Though Shin Buddhism improvised a radically new form of practice, its goal is one and the same with that of Mahayana Buddhism. The goal is to awaken to the true self as a manifestation of *dharma* or "reality-as-is." What this means may be illustrated by some popular metaphors in the Pure Land tradition.

First is the metaphor of the color gold. Down through the ages, this metal has been the most highly prized of possessions. It has also been associated with things of a spiritual nature, and each religion has found it a rich symbol. Gold adorns the ark of the covenant containing the Ten Commandments; gold is remembered by Christians as the precious gift of Magi to the newborn Jesus; the giver of gold in the Rig-Veda receives a life of light and glory; and the fifth Mohammedan Heaven in Islam is made of gold. In short, gold has been the universal symbol of that which we value most.

In Buddhism the color gold is no less precious, symbolizing supreme awakening or enlightenment. The third of the forty-eight vows, established and fulfilled by Amida Buddha, in the *Larger Sutra,* proclaims:

> May I not gain possession of perfect awakening if, once I have attained buddhahood, any one among the humans and gods in my land are not all the color of genuine gold.

In the realm of enlightened beings, the Pure Land, everyone is golden colored; that is to say, everyone without exception attains supreme awakening. Discrimination based on color, gender, age, social class, intellectual ability, and so forth are meaningless and without foundation. Each person is affirmed to become as he or she truly is, fulfilling the innate potential hidden within. All beings are assured of buddhahood through the working of dharma that realizes itself in a person.

Dharma has several connotations in South Asian religions, but in Buddhism it has two basic, interrelated meanings: dharma as "teaching" as found in the expression Buddha Dharma, and dharma as "reality-as-is" (*adhigama-dharma*). The teaching is a verbal expression of reality-as-is that consists of two aspects—the subject that realizes and the object that is realized. Together they constitute "reality-as-is"; if either aspect is lacking, it is not reality-as-is. This sense of dharma or reality-as-is is also called suchness (*tathata*) or thatness (*tattva*) in Buddhism.

The lotus flower, the second metaphor, reveals the distinctive meaning of suchness or thatness. The lotus has been an important religious symbol in the Asian world for more than five thousand years with different significations. In the Pure Land tradition it represents the uniqueness of each person, or each

reality-as-is, distinct from all others each with its own uniqueness. While supreme enlightenment symbolized by gold stresses
nondifferentiation, suchness or thatness affirms the uniqueness
of each concrete particular. This is fundamental to the Buddhist
understanding of "equality" (*samata*) which is not undifferentiated sameness but the affirmation of the suchness of the concrete particular—each flower as such, each leaf as such, each
butterfly as such, each person as such, and so on.

This varied multiplicity is foundational to the Mahayana
worldview of the interconnectedness and interdependence of life.
This multicolored splendor is expressed poetically in the *Smaller
Sutra:*

> On the surface of the pools,
> there are lotus blossoms as large as cart wheels.
> These are blue colored, with blue sheen;
> yellow colored, with yellow sheen;
> red colored, with red sheen;
> white colored, with white sheen;
> they are delicate and fragrant.

The multiple colors of the lotus blossoms, each radiating its
distinctive luster, creates the glory of the enlightened realm. This
is the realm of the Pure Land, the world of enlightenment. But
this world is not a given; it is to be realized through undergoing
a radical transformation.

This transformation is suggested in the third metaphor of
transformed rubble, based on scripture that reads: "We who are
like bits of rubble are transformed into gold." All-embracing
and nonexclusive, this path accepts everyone, even the lowliest
who are considered nothing more than "bits of rubble" in the
eyes of society. But no matter who or what one is, everyone is

transformed through the power of compassion to become authentically real as an awakened person. "Bits of rubble" is the realization of those who, illuminated by Immeasurable Light and Immeasurable Life that is Amida, are made to see their essential finitude, imperfection, and mortality. This realization may not sound too inspiring, but affirming one's basic reality is the crucial factor in the transformative process. To bring about such a transformation is the sole purpose of the Primal Vow of Amida, the working of great compassion that courses through the universe.

This metaphor of alchemical transmutation is based on the Mahayana teaching of the nonduality of samsara and nirvana, delusion and enlightenment, rubble and gold. This is not a simple identity, for it involves a dialectical tension between the two poles, between limited karmic beings and unbounded compassion. The two remain separate, yet they are one; they are one, yet always remain separate. This requires some explanation, but before we get to that let us place the Pure Land tradition in the landscape of Buddhism, relative to other schools and denominations.

THE SPIRIT OF
THE VALLEY

3

南無阿彌陀佛

The ideal of monastic Buddhism is transcendence of mundane existence, as if one were ascending to the mountaintop. In contrast, the
praxis of Pure Land Buddhism takes place by
descending into the valley, the shadow of the
mountains. We find a similar contrast in Chinese
civilization. Like monastic Buddhism, the Confucian ideal may be symbolized by the soaring
mountain peaks, manifesting the highest achievements of the literati. And like the Pure Land,
Taoism is found in the valley and lowlands, a
haven for those who do not fit into conventional
society for whatever reason. But it is in this valley
that life and creativity flourish. In the words of
Tao-te-ching:

> The Valley Spirit never dies.
> It is named the Mysterious Female.
> And the Doorway of the mysterious Female

Is the base from which Heaven and Earth
     sprang.
It is there within us all the while;
Draw upon it as you will, it never runs dry.

In the valley fecundity is nourished and dynamic creativity is born. From its depth comes the life force that creates Heaven and Earth. Immortalized as the Spirit of the Valley and identified with the feminine principle, its procreative vitality is inexhaustible. Hence, the name of this Taoist classic, the Way (*tao*) and its Power (*te*). The valley ultimately is the resting place for everything that is washed down from the mountaintop, collecting all kinds of refuse and garbage of society and welcoming the unwanted, the disappointed, and the broken.

In Japan, traditional Buddhist monasticism—whether Tendai, Shingon, or Zen—aims at the transcendence of earthly passions. Its basic precepts consist of renouncing all family ties, maintaining celibacy, mastering rigorous disciplines, avoiding contact with the opposite sex, and engaging in elaborate rituals. In contrast, Pure Land is the trans-descendence into the opposite world, the self-awakening to the immersion in the swamp of anger, jealousy, insecurity, fear, addiction, arrogance, hypocrisy. It was only natural that Pure Land teaching was originally welcomed especially by those of the lower classes, seen as unredeemable in the eyes of the privileged. But among this worthless debris and discarded refuse, a rich spirituality is cultivated, endowing a person with endless energy and boundless vitality.

Shin Buddhism comes alive for those who live in the valley and in the shadows. It challenges people to discover the ultimate meaning of life in the abyss of the darkness of ignorance. As we respond fully to the challenge, the Shin teaching helps us to negotiate our way through the labyrinth of samsaric life. The wonder of this teaching is that liberation is made available to us not because we are wise but *because* we are ignorant, limited, imperfect, and finite. In the language of Pure Land Buddhism, we who are foolish beings (*bonbu*) are transformed into the very opposite by the power of great compassion.

Honen summed up the varied paths of Buddhism in his pronouncement: "In the Path of Sages one perfects wisdom and achieves enlightenment: in the Path of Pure Land one returns to the foolish self to be saved by Amida." Religious awakening does not depend initially on who we are or what we do; rather, it is becoming attuned to the working of great compassion at the heart of existence. This attunement is realized through deep hearing (*monpo*) of the call from the depth. Nothing is required of us, other than the engagement with deep hearing. Since this is the only requirement—no precepts, no meditative practices, no doctrinal knowledge, it is known as the "easy path."

Easy path, however, only describes the simplicity of the path, not its level of difficulty to realize, for the easy path is by no means "easy." Deep hearing is a *real* challenge and *can be* a hard struggle, especially for the arrogant, because the call must *become* embodied in a person. Embodying means *living* the nembutsu from which flows the spontaneous saying of namu-amida-butsu. The actual process thus may not be so simple, as we are reminded in the Pure Land saying: "Although the path is easy, few are there to take it." The obstacles encountered are different from those pursuing monastic disciplines on the Path of Sages because one must struggle with oneself in the midst of all kinds of entanglements in society. As James Hillman points out, "The way through the world is more difficult to find than the way beyond it."

Pure Land Buddhism might suggest an otherworldly orientation, but its primary focus is on the here and now. Not the here and now grasped by the controlling ego-self, but the here and now cherished as a gift of life itself to be lived creatively and gratefully, granted us by boundless compassion. The bountifulness of great compassion makes possible our liberation from the iron cage of our own making.

HOME COMPOSTING

As part of an effort to become more environmentally conscious, my hometown of Northampton, Massachusetts, has been encouraging home composting by all the residents. After all, every little bit helps solve the ecological problems of overflowing landfills, chemical poisoning, deforestation, soil erosion, and disappearing ozone layer. Each household was given manuals on composting with detailed instructions on the waste material to use. The mixture of decaying organic substances, such as food scraps, apple and banana peelings, leftover leafy vegetables, coffee grinds, cut lawn grass, and shredded leaves will not only reduce trash but produce rich, fertile soil. As I was reading the manual, I was reminded of a Shin poem by Chisho Yanagida:

> When the soil receives waste material,
> The waste material is turned into soil.

It's not necessary to change into soil
To become part of the soil.
The soil receives whatever is given
Without making any demands.

Namu-amida-butsu receives
A person just as is.
When the nembutsu receives a person,
No matter who or what,
The person is transformed into the nembutsu,
Celebrating and blessing life.

The nembutsu takes me as I am,
Imperfect and incomplete,
With worries and problems,
And transforms everything
Into the contents of highest virtue.

The wonder of the nembutsu path is that it makes no demands upon a person to become wiser, better, or more perfect. But it does ask us to become authentically real as human beings by awakening to the boundless compassion that sustains us. In doing so we recognize our limitations and imperfections as karmic beings that are ultimately transformed into the contents of highest good. When "bits of rubble are transformed into gold," the fullness of Buddha Dharma is manifested in a person's life.

Some years ago, my wife and I were living in an apartment complex in Los Angeles with our son who was then two years old. One day, I asked him what he wanted to become when he grew up. This may seem like a trick question for a two-year-old, but he immediately shouted back, "Garbage man!" Well, I wasn't necessarily expecting him to say, "Buddhist scholar!" but his choice of profession was a bit surprising. But I remembered his fascination with the gleaming, white sanitation truck that would come rumbling by our apartment every Tuesday morning to pick up the trash cans placed on the sidewalk. As the rear of the huge truck opened up with a loud grinding sound, it swallowed up all the garbage the sanitation workers threw into it. I thought about how astounding this must be to a child—it was like a huge monster devouring food. I then said, "OK, but become the world's best *Buddhist* garbage collector!"

Up until that point, I hadn't really ever stopped to consider garbage trucks and sanitation workers, but always on the lookout for a good metaphor, I began pondering their metaphysical implications. Since the garbage we carry around with us—our ignorance, mistakes, addictions, vanities, and neuroses—are completely accepted without any questions, Amida is like a garbage collector who willingly takes the refuse and dumps them into his Pure Landfill (aptly coined by an astute friend). Since everything is biodegradable in the compassionate hands of Amida, the landfill transforms itself into nutrients that can contribute to a rich and fertile life.

A poem by Tz'u-min, the Chinese Pure Land master of the eighth century, sums up the working of true compassion:

> That Buddha, in his bodhisattva stage, made the
>   universal vow:
> When beings hear my Name and think on me, I will
>   come and welcome them.
> Not discriminating at all between the poor and the
>   rich and well born,
> Not discriminating between the inferior and highly
>   gifted;

Not choosing the learned and those who uphold pure
     precepts.
Not rejecting those who break precepts and whose evil
     karma is profound,
Solely making beings turn about and abundantly say
     the Name,
I can make bits of rubble change into gold.

As discussed in the previous chapter, "bits of rubble" is a metaphor for imperfect, unenlightened human beings who are the
primary concern of great compassion. By extension it refers to
the difficulties, conflicts, and frustrations that we also experience in life. Everything negative is transmuted into gold. The
nembutsu practicer Ichitaro experienced such a transformation whenever he encountered problems in life. He once said,
"You don't run away from your troubles and then find happiness. Rather, you no longer think of troubles as troubles.
And troubles of themselves turn into happiness, namu-amida-
butsu."

Some problems in life have no rational answers, but this
does not mean the end of the world. In fact, in an unexpected
moment of revelation a new chapter in one's life may open.
Brian Schulz, suffering from painful degenerative joint disease,
states in Mark Ian Barasch's *A Healing Path:* "When before my
desire had been to rid myself of my illness as if it were a foreign
object, an invader, I now began to treat it as part of me that was
calling out to be touched." A similar thought is echoed by Joseph Cardinal Bernardin of Chicago, who, just before he died on
November 14, 1996, said: "Death is my friend." These are
precisely the sentiment expressed in the popular Shin saying:
"Illness, too, is my good friend (*kalyanamitra*)."

Before the recycling program in my hometown, I didn't

really stop to think about garbage having any value at all. But on the Pure Land path it is those aspects of ourselves that we want to get rid of that are priceless, for they are the primary concern of great compassion that transforms them into cherished, valuable possessions.

PRIMAL VOW

5

南
無
阿
彌
陀
佛

The transformation of bits of rubble into gold is due solely to the working of the Primal Vow. Originating in the mythic past, the bodhisattva by the name of Dharmakara identified with the pains of all living beings and attempted to find solutions to human suffering. Expending countless eons of time in suprahuman resolve, reflection, and praxis, Dharmakara fulfilled the Primal Vow to save all beings. This resulted in the attainment of Buddhahood known as Amida, the Buddha of Immeasurable Light and Life. This drama of salvation is contained in the Name, namu-amida-butsu, which resounds throughout the universe.

The Primal Vow of salvation is likened to a powerful magnet that draws all beings to itself. Even if one is unaware of it or resists it, its power of attraction will eventually prevail. It is also compared to mother earth. According to Shinran,

"The vow of compassion is like the great earth, for all the Buddhas of past, present, and future throughout the ten quarters arise from it."

All people have their private dreams of success and happiness, making vows to achieve them sooner or later. The goal, however, is elusive, and the vast majority of the people rarely attain it. Now, the Primal Vow works to salvage humankind's heartbreaks and shattered dreams, transforming them into sources of a rich and full life. One then necessarily comes to realize that this unrepeatable life contains unexpected treasures and rewards. The ceaseless working of the Primal Vow continues as long as there is suffering in the world, for its primary task is performing spiritual alchemy, transforming "bits of rubble" into gold.

This Vow is "primal" (Sanskrit *purva*) in the sense that it is prior to the beginningless beginning of time, taking in all beings unconditionally. It foresees all the wishes, desires, and aspirations, as well as the failures and dejections, experienced by humanity. As such, it has prepared answers and solutions for the needs of every human being. Although the depth and scope of the working of the Primal Vow is beyond our imagination, it reaches us through the Name, namu-amida-butsu. Thus, anyone, anywhere, and anytime can intone the Name and awaken to its countless benefits.

Tradition says that it takes five hundred rebirths to be born into human life and one thousand rebirths to encounter the Buddha Dharma, but the Primal Vow precedes even these countless rebirths. Whenever I hear the astronomical numbers encountered in Buddhist literature, I think of the Japanese garden at Smith College built in 1986. Located on a gentle slope overlooking Paradise Pond at the center of the campus, the rock formations depict the life of Buddha. Symbolically represented are scenes of his birth, renunciation, enlightenment, first sermon, and parinirvana, as well as the Three Gems—Buddha, Dharma, and Sangha—and the Four Noble Truths. From the tea hut atop the garden one looks down on the waters of Paradise Pond and the Other Shore.

What makes the garden unique are the seventy tons of boulders brought in from the surrounding hills of the Connecticut River valley. Since I was curious about the age of the rocks, I invited a geologist friend to come and look at them. He approached the rocks with loving care—silently caressing the rocks, gently tapping them here and there, softly blowing away the dust. After several minutes of concentrated observation, he informed me of the two ages of the rocks that we had collected for our garden.

Some of the rocks were formed 350 to 450 million years ago—metamorphic rocks, originally ocean sediments, and plutonic igneous rocks that are magmas melted from ancient crusts. The other kind, called gneiss rocks, is at least one billion years old. By pure coincidence these billion-year-old rocks were selected for the meditative seat of Buddha's enlightenment and the reclining Buddha in the death scene. Compared to the age of these rocks, the history of humankind is not even a speck of time. Even less is the minuscule span of each human life.

One billion years is beyond our imagination, but the Primal Vow exceeds it in time and depth. Shinran speaks of its origination ten kalpas ago, or in some cases five kalpas ago. A kalpa is a unit of time, conceived by the mathematicians of ancient India who discovered the decimal system. According to one source, it is equal to a thousand cycles of Maha Yugas or 4,320,000,000 years. Another explains it by the following analogy. A warehouse, forty square miles, is full of mustard seeds. One seed is taken out once every one hundred years. The duration it takes to

empty the warehouse is one kalpa. The ten kalpas required to
fulfill the Primal Vow suggests the immensity of its profound
undertaking—how to uproot the darkness of ignorance inherent
in each human being from the beginningless beginning of time.

This darkness of ignorance is expressed by Shan-tao as follows: "Truly know that this self is a foolish being of karmic evil,
repeating birth-and-death since beginningless eons ago, forever
drowning and wandering without ever knowing the path of liberation." This ignorance is not the lack of factual knowledge but
suggests that reality is beyond the pale of conventional thinking.
Yui-en, the compiler of *Tannisho*, expresses this in the following
reflection:

> How grateful I am that Shinran expressed this in his
> own person to make us deeply realize that we do not
> know the depth of karmic evil and that we do not know
> the height of Tathagata's benevolence, all of which cause
> us to live in utter confusion. (*Tannisho* Epilogue)

Just as we cannot know the depth of karmic evil, so also we fail
to appreciate the full working of true compassion. This dual
failing, due to the limitation of our rational capacity, is the
source of unending suffering in our world.

The essence of the Primal Vow is boundless compassion,
articulated in the eighteenth of the forty-eight vows fulfilled by
Bodhisattva Dharmakara as a condition of attaining Buddhahood. According to the *Larger Sutra*, used extensively in East
Asia, this fundamental vow proclaims:

> If, when I attain Buddhahood, the sentient beings of the
> ten quarters with sincere mind, joyful trust, and aspira-
> tion for birth in my land and saying my Name perhaps

even ten times, should not be born there, may I not attain the supreme enlightenment. Excluded are those who commit the five transgressions and those who slander the right dharma.

The key terms in the vow—sincere mind, joyful trust, and aspiration for birth—are known as the Three Minds. Traditionally, the three were considered to be the proper attitudes necessary for religious faith. Shinran, however, reversed this and made clear that the three are qualities of Amida that infuse the life of each person. They form the content of true entrusting that enables a person to become true, real, and sincere.

The sincere mind in the Primal Vow has nothing to do with the mind of a karma-bound being that is devoid of that which is true and real. Rather it denotes the mind of Amida, which enters the defiled mind of a sentient being. This results in true entrusting with joy and spontaneity. The sincere mind of Amida working in a person also awakens the aspiration for transcendence, or birth in the Pure Land. The goal of transcendence is to become a Buddha, endowed with wisdom and compassion, in order to work for the salvation of all beings.

This radical reinterpretation of the Three Minds culminates in what is known as the fulfillment of the eighteenth vow:

All sentient beings, having heard the Name, entrust themselves and rejoice in one thought-moment. This is the result of the sincere mind of the Buddha. If they aspire to be born in that Buddha land, they will attain new birth and reside in the stage of non-retrogression. Excluded are those who commit the five transgressions and slander the dharma.

Both of the scriptural passages quoted above attest to the all-inclusive, boundless compassion of the Buddha Amida. The sincere mind of Amida working in sentient beings assures their attainment of nonretrogression, the state of being that prevents backsliding into samsara. But the exclusion of transgressors and slanderers seems to contradict the absolute nature of compassion. Those excluded are people guilty of the five great evils: doing violence to father, mother, and monks; spilling blood from the Buddha's body; and creating dissension in the Sangha. Also excluded are those who slander the Buddha Dharma, an even greater offense because it negates any access to a salvific source. This so-called exclusion clause had posed a hermeneutical problem for Pure Land masters down through the ages. Various explanations were given to justify this exclusion.

Shinran summed up the types of people mentioned in the exclusion clause and simplified it to the following: "People who look down on teachers and who speak ill of masters commit slander of the dharma. Those who speak ill of their parents are guilty of the five great offenses." The existential question for him came down to the basic question: Who among us is not guilty of criticizing our teachers and talking back to our parents?

Now, Shinran understood the exclusion clause in relation to his own predicament and understood its purpose to be twofold. First of all, it is an injunction against the unethical life. Since the offenses are grave, he warns that salvation may be impossible for those who commit them. Second, however, for those who are already guilty, like himself, the exclusion clause highlights the very object of the Primal Vow of compassion. In truth, the salvation of such an evil doer is an indispensable component of the Primal Vow; without it the Vow remains unfulfilled and Buddhahood unrealized. Shinran makes the point simply: "By revealing the gravity of these two transgressions, these words make us realize that the beings in all quarters of the universe will be born in the Pure Land *without exception* [emphasis added]."

In the Epilogue to the *Tannisho* Shinran gratefully affirms this fact in his famous confessional:

> When I ponder on the compassionate vow of Amida, established through five kalpas of profound thought, it was for myself, Shinran, alone. Because I am a being burdened so heavily with karma, I feel even more deeply grateful to the Primal Vow which is decisively made to save me.

Down through the centuries, countless people have replaced Shinran's name with their own and recited this confessional, grateful for having personally encountered the compassionate Vow in the midst of samsaric life.

NEMBUTSU: THE NAME-THAT-CALLS

6

南無阿彌陀佛

When my friend, Teruo, first posed the question about karma to me, it was just another concept among many that I was studying. It had nothing to do with my life, and even less with the questions that would eventually consume me: Who am I? Where did my life come from? Where is it going? I soon began to realize that the whole message of the Buddha is directed to answering these fundamental questions about the self, this self bound by a karmic past and yearning for liberation and freedom.

The Pure Land response is contained in "namu-amida-butsu." This is the *nembutsu* that originally implied "contemplating the Buddha" but today more commonly means "saying the Name of Amida Buddha." The two are distinguished as meditative nembutsu and recitative nembutsu. What is the significance of this invocation of the Name of Amida?

Central to the nembutsu is the awakening to human finitude and limitations, the awareness of the darkness of ignorance (*avidya*) that gives rise to greed, anger, and folly. The *namu* component of nembutsu expresses this finitude. This realization of *namu*—lost, rootless, and directionless—is brought to awareness by *amida-butsu*, boundless and endless compassion that enfolds it. *Amida* means "immeasurable," that which is not measurable and beyond conceptual understanding.

Amida combines the dual connotation of its Sanskrit originals, *Amitabha*, Immeasurable Light, and *Amitayus*, Immeasurable Life. *Butsu* is the Japanese rendition for Buddha. Thus, illuminated by the Buddha of Immeasurable Light and Immeasurable Life, I am made to realize my reality as a karma-bound being—limited, imperfect, and mortal—contained within boundless compassion. In the full acknowledgment of my finitude, of my karmic bondage, liberation and freedom are realized.

The saying of nembutsu confirms the boundless, endless life (*amida-butsu*) in which the insecure self (*namu*) finds itself at home. Human reason cannot fathom the fullness of living namu-amida-butsu, for much of it is beyond our conscious awareness. On the conscious level, however, there is constant tension between the awareness of a limited being, *namu*, asserting itself at every occasion, and the openness of compassion, *amida-butsu*, providing the space for us to be ourselves. But this tension ultimately culminates in supreme enlightenment through the power of the Primal Vow.

Philosophically speaking, the nembutsu is the self-articulation of fundamental reality. As such, the saying of the Name contains the alpha and omega of the Buddhist soteriological path. The Name is vibrant with mythic significance, full of indicators that transcend ordinary ways of thinking: Dharmakara Bodhisattva's original vows identifying with human suffering, fulfillment of the multiple vows making our liberation an accomplished fact, the consequent attainment of Buddhahood, and supreme enlightenment of all beings, past, present, and future. We might understand this story, rich with religiosity, in a simple, direct way.

The words and concepts of everyday language are useful and necessary for life, but once their usefulness ends, the words disappear. In contrast, the Name, namu-amida-butsu, is the source of creative life, the power that affirms reality-as-is. Each time it is intoned, vital life is experienced. What does this mean? Through the working of the Name, we are made to become aware of ourselves as limited, finite beings (*namu*), yet secure within the sustaining power of boundless compassion (*amida-butsu*). As human beings we are made to become true, real, and sincere through the operative functioning of the Name. When we thus em-*body* the Name, Amida is right here. Apart from intoning the Name, there is no Amida. The Name is Amida Buddha. The Name is reality-as-is.

Different usages of the Name are found in religions all over the world from prehistoric times to the present. It is utilized as magical spells, charms, mantras, incantations, and ritual invocations. Common among them is the fact that the Name is seen as possessing some kind of power. Thus, it has utility value, serving a variety of human needs: curing illness, securing health, bringing good fortune, overcoming death, destroying enemy, and promising eternal life.

In contrast, the primary function of the Name in Shin Buddhism is its truth value, it brings about the realization of reality-as-is. In brief, the Name has no miraculous powers, it has nothing to do with ecstatic visions, it never promises any material benefits, and it makes no pretense about solving every worldly problem. The fundamental purpose of the Name as namu-amida-butsu is awakening to the incomparable worth of this unrepeatable life, this limited, finite life that is inseparable from boundless, infinite life.

One of the closest parallels to this nembutsu practice in world religions is the Jesus Prayer of the Eastern Orthodox Church. *The Way of the Pilgrim* urges people to undertake the ceaseless prayer, "Lord Jesus Christ have mercy on me." At one point the pilgrim is required to repeat the prayer twelve thousand times a day.

> Ceaseless prayer is to call upon the Name of God always, whether a man is conversing, or sitting down, or walking, or making something, or eating, whatever he may be doing, in all places and at all times, he ought to call upon God's Name.

This reminds us of the daily practice of Tao-ch'o, who is said to have repeated the nembutsu seventy thousand times a day. Honen also encouraged the constant saying of the Name; and he, too, is reported to have undertaken sixty thousand or seventy thousand invocations daily.

A more sophisticated interpretation of the Jesus Prayer appears in a small tract, *On the Invocation of the Name of Jesus,* a joint product of the Anglican and Orthodox Churches. In this work reciting the Name of Jesus is understood in three basic ways: as a contemplative act pursued in a quiet setting, as a method of contacting the Person of Jesus, and as a form of asceticism, requiring forgetfulness of self and the banishing of sinful images. It also warns against "verbal idolatry," using the Name for utilitarian purposes.

While Shin Buddhism upholds the centrality of recitative nembutsu, it has nothing to do with the number of invocations.

What is crucial is the quality of the heart inherent in each saying, the purity of response to the call of the Buddha of Immeasurable Light and Life. Thus, even a single utterance, or even the "thought of wanting to say the nembutsu," is sufficient. No condition of any kind is placed on a person; the only thing required is deep hearing, the repeated hearing of the calling of nembutsu.

Since the nembutsu is regarded as the self-articulation of reality, Shin Buddhists do not consider "namu-amida-butsu" to be connected to any particular language—Sanskrit, Chinese, Japanese, or others—although historically it is derived from the Sanskrit. As the ultimate religious symbol, the Name is the primary object of devotional worship. Namu-amida-butsu, written on a scroll and placed on the altar, is the central image. It is preferred over sculpted or painted figures of Amida. Since reality becomes manifest wherever and whenever the Name is intoned, it is clearly not an abstract concept, intellectually devised, nor is it a signifier related to the signified. Ultimately, the nembutsu is the creative life force that becomes manifest in a person, embodied in thought, action, and speech.

When Honen was on his deathbed, his disciples gathered around him and expressed sadness and regret that their master did not build any temples or monuments by which they could remember him. Great monks and priests in the past all had erected huge temples and founded monasteries, and their life and deeds were celebrated with elaborate memorial services at these sites. Honen lived in a simple hermitage, his gates always open to the people. He rejected the building of edifices, and on his deathbed said, "Wherever the nembutsu is intoned, there is my temple."

As a form of religious practice, however, recitative nembutsu has two functions. First, it voices our deepest wish to go beyond the ego-self and to become true, real, and sincere as a human being. When this actually begins to take place, we immediately encounter an obstacle, our own ego-self, and come to see that it has already been accomplished in the timeless past for each of us from the side of Amida Buddha. Second, we then respond to the Name-that-calls with gratitude, a gratitude so profound that ordinary language cannot express it. Hence, the only recourse is the nembutsu, the creative word that comes from the deepest source of life itself. In either case, the Name-that-calls comes from the depth and touches us, and when we respond with our whole being, we awaken from the slumber of self-delusion and open our eyes to the endless wonder that is life.

Once a student in my class on Buddhist thought at Smith College wrote an essay, revealing the significance of "calling" in her own experience. The incident occurred during a hiking trip into the Grand Canyon. With several friends Julia took a long trek into the canyon. In due time she lagged behind and found herself all alone. Suddenly she realized that she was lost in unfamiliar terrain. Julia yelled out the names of her friends, but only their echoes resounded in the canyon. An eerie silence prevailed.

With the coming of dusk, the air became chillier, and she tried to keep herself warm as best she could. Surely her friends would come back looking for her, she thought, but as time passed and darkness descended, there was no sign of a search party. The night air became colder, wild animals howled incessantly, and suspicious rustling in the bushes struck fear.

Then in the night stillness, she heard faint human voices in the distance. As the minutes passed, the voices became stronger. She could hear movements in the darkness approaching her. The search party was calling out to her; soon the calling became clearer and clearer. She distinctly heard the calling directed to her; and she in response yelled back to identify herself. Though she couldn't see the search party in the darkness, their calling out affirmed their presence and ensured her rescue. As Julia responded to the call, she was no longer afraid. In hearing her name called and calling in return, she felt strong in body and mind. Her whole being was transformed from one of total confusion to one of complete well-being. The nembutsu functions in our life in a similar way, so I translate it into English as the Name-that-calls.

The Chinese and Japanese character for "name" consists of two ideographs: "dusk" and "mouth." When we are lost in the darkness, someone calls out and identifies himself or herself by name. In fact, the Japanese word for "dusk," *tasogare*, means "who is there?" In the darkness we hear a name, confirm it, and all is right with the world. Although we may be groping in the darkness, once we hear the Name, we are brought out of the darkness into an open field of bright sunshine. This clarity enables us to see ourselves as we are, free of subjectivity. This insight into self is the noetic core at the heart of nembutsu. Let me illustrate this with a simple example.

At bedtime as a little boy begins to go to sleep in the dark, he sees monsters in the room and cries out, "Mommy, Mommy." The mother comes into the room, turns on the light switch, and comforts the child, saying, "Look, there's no monster here." He is relieved, the mother turns off the light and leaves the room. Comforted, he tries to go back to sleep again, but in the darkness the child sees monsters jumping around in the room, and full of fear he begins to cry. The mother rushes back to the room, and this time remains with him in the darkness. She then actually notices ominous figures dancing around on the wall; they are shadows thrown by the streetlight, swaying trees blown by the wind. The mother wakes up the boy, turns on the light, and shows him that his fear is real but unfounded. The light is turned off, the child fully understands, and he soon falls asleep, softly murmuring, "Mommy, Mommy." At the core of nembutsu experience is a noetic element that enables us to see things as they are, so that we are no longer fooled or agitated by delusions.

Such is the function of the Name, the self-articulation of reality that comes to be embodied in a person. Ultimate reality in Buddhism is called *dharmakaya*; it is beyond description, imagination, and conception. Since it transcends the horizon of our understanding, it reveals itself in our world as the Name, namu-amida-butsu, making itself accessible to anyone at any time. To truly hear the Name-that-calls is to be led out of darkness into the light of day.

When we thus realize reality, it is more basic than simply being "religious," or being "good." For this reason Shinran asserts:

> The saying of nembutsu is neither a religious practice nor a good act. Since it is practiced without any calculation, it is "non-practice." Since it is also not a good created by my calculation, it is "non-good." Since it is nothing but Other Power, completely separate from self-power, it is neither a religious practice nor a good act on the part of the practicer. (*Tannisho* VIII)

How does the ordinary person understand this working of the Name? How does one respond to the Name-that-calls? Among the many responses, here is one that is frequently quoted with minor variations:

> Although the voice that calls
> Namu-amida-butsu is mine,
> It is the call of my dear parent,
> Saying, "Come as you are!"

The Japanese original for "dear parent" is *oya-sama*. This term that makes no distinction between father and mother conveys a much warmer and more intimate feeling than the English word parent. Our parent as *oya-sama* always welcomes us back without any conditions attached, saying "Come as you are!" It makes no difference, whether we are depressed, lonely, angry, feel rejected, thirsting for love, or fearful of the unknown. Great compassion awaits us with an open arm. Namu-amida-butsu is the beckoning call, "Come, just as you are!"

This openhearted welcome is quietly described by Koshin Ogui in an article carried in the Cleveland Buddhist Temple Newsletter. He relates an experience he once had of returning home from a trip. In his absence the answering machine had recorded four phone calls from the same person. The message was, "Jesus is the only savior. Believe in him and you'll be saved. Love him and you'll be loved. Anyone who does not believe in him will go to hell." Ogui comments:

> What do you say about this message. I don't know why, but then I recalled meeting with my mother on my recent trip to Japan. I hadn't seen her for five years. As soon as I opened the door to the house where I was born, there she was standing right in front of me. She didn't say anything much, but she held my hand and with tears in her eyes, she said, "You came home." Isn't that nice, to be welcomed without any justification, whether I believe in her or not, or love her or not. I

realize that I have always been living in her love. I am grateful. Namu-amida-butsu.

In ordinary language namu-amida-butsu is saying, "I have arrived, I have come home." Thus, Shin Buddhists call this the truly settled state.

OTHER POWER

7

The working of the Primal Vow, the compassion
of the Buddha of Immeasurable Light and Life, is
called Other Power. But this "other" is not op-
posed to "self" in the dualistic sense. This becomes clear when we understand that the starting
point of Pure Land Buddhism is not Amida Buddha but Dharmakara Bodhisattva. As a bodhisattva, Dharmakara saw deeply into the immense
sufferings of all beings, identified with them
completely, discerned their causes, found a way
to eliminate them, and prepared the practice for
each being to attain liberation. When this Primal
Vow was fulfilled and perfected, the Buddha of
Immeasurable Light and Life became a reality.

Dharmakara Bodhisattva is with each of us
right now in our struggles, sharing our pains and
our hopes, remaining by our side, and helping us
in our spiritual journey. Dharmakara will not rest
until the story of our own life reaches full realiza-

tion with our own liberation and freedom. When we attain this liberation and freedom, then Amida Buddha becomes a living reality. This process is encapsulated in the living of nembutsu, "namu-amida-butsu." *Namu* is the lost, wandering self, seeking a way to realize its fullest potential. *Amida-butsu* or Amida Buddha is great compassion that calls all lost and delusory beings to itself. When fully grounded in such a compassion, one's flowering as a true, real, and sincere person takes place naturally and spontaneously.

Other Power, then, is the *working* of great compassion that gives itself completely to each form of life. It is beyond the ordinary comprehension of the small-minded, entangled with all kinds of false discriminations. Other Power thus should not be regarded as an object within the conventional subject-object framework. It operates at the very foundation of life, nullifying all our dualistic calculations (*hakarai*).

This appreciation of the "other" as nondual is expressed experientially by Saichi (1850–1933), a so-called *myokonin*, a person of humble origin but penetrating insight:

> In Other Power
> There is no self-power
> There is no other-power
> All is Other Power.

For Saichi, self-power and Other Power are arbitrary distinctions made from the side of human beings. Since the compassion of Amida, beyond our conceptual grasp, is boundless, it is called great compassion (*karuna*). This compassion endows wisdom (*prajna*) in each existence as it is without any judgment. The adjective "great" connotes the mind and heart of the Buddha that embraces all kinds of dualities—self and other, good and bad, young and old, life and death, and so on—transforming them into sources of dynamic, creative life. How can one appreciate the working of Other Power?

In his remarkable book, *Thoughts Without a Thinker*, which integrates Western psychotherapy with basic Buddhism, Mark Epstein writes:

> Instead of running from difficult emotions (or hanging on to enticing ones), the practitioner of bare attention becomes able to *contain* any reaction: making space for it, but not completely identifying with it because of the concomitant presence of nonjudgmental awareness.

This is an excellent description of what might take place in meditative practice. One experiences a wide, open space, free of any kind of value judgment, to contend with difficult emotions. A similar freedom and openness is found in Shin Buddhism but with radical differences.

The boundless space is provided us by the great compassion of the Buddha of Immeasurable Light and Life. This compassion is not only nonjudgmental but understands fully all of our defiled passions: "All this the Buddha already knew and called us foolish beings of blind passion. Thus, when we realize that the compassionate vow of Other Power is for beings like ourselves, the vow becomes even more reliable and dependable." (*Tannisho* IX) This point is made quietly and clearly by David Ignatow:

> I am, and so Buddha and I are not one,
> but this is for my human self
> to know that he exists and I exist
> in his eyes and am understood.

This compassion and wisdom of Amida empowers us, enabling us to cope with all kinds of difficult challenges in life.

The empowerment frees us to openly acknowledge our limitations and imperfections, even our addictions and neuroses. Through the working of Other Power, we become ourselves truly, to embrace our feelings without regrets, remorse, or feeling guilty. Because of this space and understanding provided us, the writings of Shin Buddhists abound with pure emotions fully exposed—joy, sadness, humor, sorrow, anger, foolishness, repentance, gratitude. Liberated from the lingering effects of our karmic past, we move forward in life positively and creatively.

What all this means may be illustrated by the life of a Shin Buddhist woman by the name of Haru Matsuda, who left many religious poems to express her deepest insights into life. Mrs. Matsuda was one of many Japanese immigrants to settle in Kona, Hawaii, at the turn of the century. They formed a community around a Shin Buddhist temple, known as the Kona Hongwanji. Nurtured by her faith, she expressed her appreciation in short poems as is the Japanese custom. Among the countless poems that she wrote are the following:

> Embraced by true compassion,
> I vowed never to complain;
> Thinking thus,
> Again I complained.

> Rubbing my eyes in the morning,
> I began complaining;
> Out jumped Namu-amida-butsu,
> And I really woke up.

Living under severe economic difficulties in an alien, hostile world, Mrs. Matsuda and her family toiled in the coffee fields of Kona. She worked from sunrise to sunset, while tending to the needs of a large family. Her life was filled with hardships, disappointments, and complaints, yet she endured and flourished, having been infused by the compassion of Amida. The compassionate working awakened her eyes to human finitude—limited, imperfect, and mortal—contained within the all-sustaining power of Amida. Having been shown her true self and grateful for this insight, she vowed never to complain. But in that very instant, she found herself complaining. She was again shown her true nature, but at that same instant realized that she had already been accepted by great compassion. In the words of Shinran, "All this the Buddha already knew and called us foolish beings of blind passion."

The second poem is even more to the point. Getting up in the morning, Mrs. Matsuda must have felt the awesome tasks ahead of her, and she began to complain. At that very moment, "out jumped Namu-amida-butsu." Through accumulated years of deep hearing, the nembutsu had become part of her subconscious. Now it had surfaced to reveal her true reality. Namu-amida-butsu affirms each *namu*—lost, confused, and complaining—within the great compassion of *amida-butsu*, Immeasurable Light and Life. Each saying of nembutsu releases us into a boundless and limitless universe.

When namu-amida-butsu struck her, she really woke up, not only to prepare for the day's work but to the reality of the human condition. She now affirmed her limitations, not as a bondage but as a liberating moment to go deeper into true and real life. With the wisdom and power endowed her, Mrs. Matsuda overcame all kinds of adversities to bring up fine children, showed compassion for the less fortunate, and contributed to enhance the life of the community.

With a lifetime of deep hearing, Mrs. Matsuda became a truly awakened human being. It enabled her to live authentically, having come to know herself thoroughly, rather than maintaining a superficial life filled with false expectations. She was fully aware of her self-delusion, not because she was especially wise or enlightened, but because her true nature had been illuminated by Immeasurable Light and Immeasurable Life. This made her the completely liberated person, as described by Shinran:

> In the person of nembutsu opens up the great path of unobstructed freedom. The reason is that the gods of heaven and earth bow before the practicer of true entrusting, and those of the world of demons and rival paths cannot obstruct the way. The consequences of karmic evil cannot bear fruit, nor does any form of good equal it. Thus, it is called the great path of unobstructed freedom. (*Tannisho* VII)

The liberated person must live out the consequences of past karma, but they no longer become burdens and no negative future karma is produced.

SELF-POWER

8

南無阿彌陀佛

The term self-power, contrasted to Other Power, should not be thought of as negating self-reliance in everyday life. To become a mature, independent adult, we must rely on the powers developed within oneself—rational, psychological, and intuitive. It is within the realm of the religious quest that self-power becomes a real problem.

According to Shinran, self-power becomes manifest in several ways. First, whenever one is "conscious of doing good" in whatever form, including religious practice, even in the saying of nembutsu, self-power is at work. Unaware of the hidden, ego-centered agenda, a person becomes self-righteous and arrogant, passing judgments on others as good or bad.

Second, whenever one believes in one's ability to "amending confusion in . . . acts, words, and thoughts" through some means, such as meditative practice, self-power is at work. One then turns to other Buddhas and deities for supplication, and engages in practices other than the nembutsu. One relies solely on one's own whims as to what is conducive to the religious life.

Third, whenever one becomes prideful in the ability to know oneself, this is the working of self-power. This includes the claim to fully recognize the limitation, imperfection, and fallibility of oneself through the power of rational self-reflection alone.

Finally, when one's religious practice, no matter how committed and dedicated, becomes ineffectual and unproductive, self-power has reached a dead end. It is at this time that the self is opened up to the working of Other Power that is all-pervasive and all-sustaining.

In everyday life, self-power manifests itself in unconscious, deep-rooted egocentric impulses. We rarely notice this, because our eyes are turned outward and we cannot see ourselves. We constantly judge and criticize others, completely unaware of our own superficial self-knowledge. This ignorance leads to all kinds of unnecessary turmoil in our personal lives and in the world. As Carl Jung once wrote, "How can anyone see straight when he does not even see himself and that darkness which he himself carries unconsciously into all his dealing."

A simple example illustrates how the calculating ego-self works when it thinks that it is doing something good. The local hospital in my hometown has an annual fund drive at the end of each year. Since I have been a beneficiary of its excellent services several times, I make it a point to send my annual contribution. At the end of each year the final report of their fund-raising campaign is announced with the donors' names listed according to different categories of giving. Despite whatever gratitude may have helped initially motivate me to give, the first thing I do when receiving this report is to make sure my name is listed, spelled correctly, and placed in the right category of giving.

One year the hospital development office announced that it would give plastic digital clocks as a token of appreciation to every donor. Having made my donation, I waited for the gift to arrive. I waited and waited. Almost six weeks I waited, but it never came. So, one day I could wait no longer and decided to call the office. In a polite voice I said, "Although I myself don't care whether I get my digital clock or not, I thought that you should know that some of us haven't received it yet. If we don't get it, you might not get any donation next year!" What I actually wanted to say was a little more blunt—"Hey, I didn't get my clock yet. If you don't send me one pronto, no donation next year!" Two days later the much-desired cheap plastic clock came in the mail. It stopped working in a few months. Somehow, this was not terribly fulfilling.

As I reflected on this incident, I asked myself, For whom did I make the donation? Obviously, it wasn't for the sake of the hospital or its services—it was purely for my own self-indulgence. My ultimate concern is not the hospital but my insatiable desire for recognition, even if it arrives only in the form of some fifty-cent electronic device. My good intention is clouded because I am always "conscious of doing good."

The myokonin Kichibei (1803–81) was a peddler of deep faith. People turned to him when they had questions regarding Shin faith. He made his points by referring to simple, everyday examples. Once he illustrated the stubborn nature of self-power by the following story.

Although fish that live in the ocean live in salty, salty water, the salt never gets into its body. If I were to explain the reason, it's because the fish is alive. But if you salt dead fish that has been landed, the salt goes right into the body to preserve it. And no matter how you try to take the saltiness out, the fish remains salty. Well, we're like fish, living every day immersed in the Buddha Dharma, and yet the Dharma never seeps into our life. Why is that? It's because our ego-self is still alive, quivering with self-power.

Self-power rejects the teaching of the Buddha as irrelevant and meaningless for our everyday life. As long as self-power is alive and well, the ego-self resists the Buddha Dharma, putting up all kinds of defenses. But sooner or later, the time will come when we will all realize the bankruptcy of self-power. When we do so, the dharma will seep into our body and mind to infuse a new and vital sense of life in us.

THE QUEST

9

南無阿彌陀佛

Self-power does not negate the effort that is required to progress on the path of awakening.
Hidden within the so-called easy path of Pure
Land Buddhism is the great tradition of self-
cultivation (*shugyo*) in the Asian tradition. Self-
cultivation disciplines both body and mind,
builds character and inner strength, curbs willfulness, and draws out the fullest potential of a
person. It is central to Confucian educational
process, Taoist psychosomatic training, Buddhist
praxis based on precepts, contemplation, and
wisdom, and the arts whether it be calligraphy,
archery, painting, tea ceremony, floral arranging,
or other cultural achievements.

Self-cultivation is the driving force in a person's attempt to live the highest ethical life, not
in words but in deeds. It is at the core of the
quest for authenticity as a human being in the
diverse paths of spirituality. In all such strivings

inevitably one is made aware of human finitude, of our reality as a karmic being—limited, imperfect, mortal. This experiential process is at the heart of Shin Buddhism, and if we miss it, the result is a superficial and distorted view of the Pure Land path. In Shin Buddhism self-cultivation is a matter of inner discipline and not of outward form which is evident to outsiders, such as sitting meditation. Consequently, it is never highlighted but it is nonetheless an essential part of "seeking the Way."

We are brought to the gates of Shin Buddhism by different routes. For some of us it is fortunate karmic circumstances from the past, frequently beyond our choice; and for others it may be due to encountering good teachers who inspire us on our quest. Some will turn to the Shin path because of unexpected tragedies or moments of sudden illumination. We will then begin to ask tentative questions about Amida Buddha, Pure Land, Primal Vow, foolish self, true entrusting. This initial stage of "listening" to the Buddha Dharma leads to further questions, as one tries to relate them to everyday life. We then become dissatisfied with purely objective questions and the extraneous answers they invite. Thus begins the next stage of engagement with "deep hearing" (monpo).

The questions become deeply personal and existential. Who am I? Where did my life come from? Where is it going? What is the purpose of my life? How do I cope with death and dying? In trying to fathom the answers we struggle to contend with oneself, with one's own darkness of ignorance, with one's self-delusions. Perseverance and effort become necessary in the struggle to understand. Regardless of the school, Buddhism regards effort to be central to the religious life. It is basic in the Noble Eightfold Path of Theravada Buddhism: right seeing, right thought, right speech, right action, right livelihood, right effort, right reflection, right meditation. In the Six Perfections of

Mahayana Buddhism it occupies an even more important place: generosity, self-discipline, patience, effort, meditation, and wisdom. In Shin Buddhism effort is manifested in the commitment to deep hearing, even if it means passing through the "great ball of fire of the three thousand worlds."

The process of "listening" to the teaching is conducted within the subject and object framework: the one who listens exists separate from the teaching that is taught. Yet the accumulation of listening eventually induces a gradual change in the subconscious, whereby the subject-object duality becomes weakened. One then enters the realm of deep hearing of the Buddha Dharma, such that one begins to discover one's true self in the teaching. In fact, the extent of deep hearing determines the degree of self-knowledge from shallow to profound. If a Shin Buddhist undertakes any form of meditative practice, it would be for the sole purpose of deep hearing.

The core of deep hearing is nonduality, whereby the subject and object become one. All vestiges of conceptualized duality disappear, whether centered on the subject or the object. As an example of nonduality centered on the subject we turn to a well-known verse from T. S. Eliot's *Four Quartets:*

> Music heard so deeply
> that it is not heard at all,
> but you are the music
> while the music lasts.

Here is deep hearing in which the music is no longer an "object"; rather it forms the total content of the subject at that moment. The subject-object framework vanishes in the experiential depth of listening. Of course, once that moment disappears, subject and object are again separate.

A similar experience of nonduality, this time centered on the object, is found in a quotation ascribed to Cézanne. Summing up his art, he said, "The landscape paints itself through me, and I am its consciousness." Here the landscape covers the horizon of experience, taking in the "subject" into itself. No separation exists between the scenery and Cézanne. But once he stops painting, he is back in the world of subject-object duality.

In contrast to these temporary experiences of nonduality, deep hearing on the Shin path leads to a radical and permanent change in a person. Having undergone tremendous struggle and ultimate awakening, a person never loses what has been gained. The complete embodying of the Buddha Dharma gives birth to a new selfhood, wisdom and compassion mature naturally. There is no turning back. Hence, this is known as the state of nonretrogression.

As we have pointed out, since the transformation in deep hearing is an internal process and has no outward form, it is not evident to outsiders. But it requires just as much (if not more) dedication and effort than other forms of religious practice. A spiritual struggle takes place within one's inner life, the struggle being an inevitable prelude to any authentic form of liberation and freedom. But that is not all.

Since the ultimate awakening is beyond human calculation and control, there is a letting go on the religious path. In the language of Shin Buddhism there occurs a release of self-power by virtue of the working of Other Power. In fact, one of the definitions that Shinran gives for Other Power is "that which is devoid of calculations" (hakarai), suggesting a spontaneous living, free of any kind of willfulness. In Rinzai Zen this entire process consists of three stages: accumulation, the relentless quest to solve a koan-riddle; saturation, total immersion into the koan; and explosion, the breakthrough into liberation and freedom. We find a similar process in the creative act.

In pottery making, for example, the potter must devote time, energy, and concentration in producing a work of art. Having exerted one's total effort in molding pottery, one places it in a kiln for firing where everything is left up to the mercy of unseen forces. The outsider sees only the finished product but never the work involved in this entire process. In a well-known work on Japanese folk art, *The Unknown Craftsman,* the world-famous potter Shoji Hamada states:

> If a kiln is small, I might be able to control it completely, that is to say, my own self can become a controller, a master of the kiln. But man's own self is but a small thing after all. When I work at the large kiln, the power of my own self becomes so feeble that it cannot control it adequately. It means that for the large kiln, the power that is beyond me is necessary. Without the mercy of such an invisible power I cannot get good pieces. One of the reasons why I wanted to have a large kiln is because I want to be a potter, if I may, who works more in grace than in his own power. You know nearly all the best pots were done in a huge kiln.

In Shin language the potter's self-power is given up completely to the working of Other Power. But this should not be understood simply in dualistic terms, for self-power and Other Power work together. Without the efforts of self-power, Other Power could not work its magic; and without Other Power, self-power remains unproductive.

In spite of different vocabularies, self-power and Other Power working together is also the foundation of Zen. One of the leading contemporary teachers of Soto Zen, Kosho Uchiyama, describes the goal of sitting meditation as "the throwing away of calculating ways of thinking which supposes that as long as there's an aim there must be a target." He then explains:

> We just sit in the midst of this contradiction where, although we aim, we can never perceive hitting the mark. We just sit in the midst of this contradiction that is absolutely ridiculous when we think about it with our small mind. In our zazen, it is precisely at the point where our small, foolish self remains unsatisfied, or completely bewildered, that immeasurable natural life beyond the thoughts of that self functions. It is precisely at the point where we become completely lost that life operates and the power of buddha is actualized.

The relentless practice of "just sitting" (*shikan taza*) undertaken by the small self, the foolish self, sooner or later reaches its limits in self-power. When this occurs, then, the awareness of a deeper "immeasurable natural life" comes alive. This is none other than the great compassion of Buddha that supports the sitting practice of the Zen student.

Such an appreciation has deep roots in the thought of Dogen, the thirteenth-century founder of Soto Zen. In an essay entitled "Birth and Death," he writes: "When you simply release and forget both your body and your mind and throw yourself into the house of buddha, and when functioning comes from the direction of the buddha and you go in accord with it, then with no strength needed and no thought expended, freed from birth and death, you become Buddha. Then there can be no obstacle in any man's mind."

The functioning that comes from the Buddha is none other than the working of Other Power. The same understanding runs through such well-known phrases as "oneness of practice and attainment" or "practice pursued on the ground of enlightenment." Attainment or enlightenment is the ground of great compassion that ensures fruitful results in religious practice. When this is neglected or forgotten, the unenlightened self runs amok, resulting in a proliferation of self-anointed gurus and pseudo-Buddhists.

UNHINDERED LIGHT

10

Working together with the Name to cultivate spirituality is Unhindered Light. Shinran states that the truly religious life is nurtured by the Name as our compassionate father and Light as our compassionate mother. We have already clarified the significance of the Name but what is the function of Light? How is it related to our practice of deep hearing?

In Buddhism Light illumines the karma-bound self and brings about its transformation. It is the "form" taken by wisdom (*prajna*) to liberate us from self-delusion. Just as love is abstract until it is realized in relation to a concrete "form" of a particular person—mother, father, child, lover, friend, or sibling—so also wisdom is abstract until it touches us in the "form" of Light to illuminate our existence. In the words of Shinran:

南無阿彌陀佛

This Tathagata is light. Light is none other than wisdom; wisdom is the form of light. Wisdom is, in addition, formless; hence this Tathagata is the Buddha of inconceivable light. This Tathagata fills the countless worlds in the ten quarters, and so is called the "Buddha of boundless light." Further, Bodhisattva Vasubandhu has given the name, "Tathagata of unhindered light filling the ten quarters."

In East Asia the term Tathagata is used as a synonym of Buddha and means "One who has come from the realm of thusness (reality-as-is)." Since nothing can obstruct the working of the Tathagata, it is also referred to as the Unhindered Light. The light of the sun and moon illuminates the world, but it does not penetrate objects and casts shadows. In contrast, Unhindered Light penetrates even the hardest substance in the world, the ego-shell of karmic beings, and never casts shadows. Nothing can obstruct its illumination.

> The light dispels the darkness of ignorance;
> Thus Amida is called "Buddha of the Light of
>   Wisdom."
> All the Buddhas and sages of the three vehicles
> Together offer their praise.

Alfred Bloom, the author of *Shinran's Gospel of Pure Grace*, describes Shinran's religious thought as the theology of light. This is a very apt description, for the Pure Land scriptures are filled with abundant references to Light. The *Smaller Sutra*, for example, states: "This Buddha's beaming light is measureless. It shines without obstruction into buddha-fields in the ten directions.

Therefore, he is called Amida." And the *Contemplation Sutra* gives us an elaborate, graphic imagery:

> The buddha Amida possesses eighty-four thousand physical characteristics, each having eighty-four thousand secondary marks of excellence. Each secondary mark emits eighty-four thousand rays of light; each light shines universally upon the lands of ten directions, embracing and not forsaking those who are mindful of the buddha.

Shinran also speaks of the Buddha as Twelve Lights, descriptive of the different dimensions of the working of wisdom. They include such Buddhas as Blazing Light, Immaculate Light, Wisdom Light, Uninterrupted Light, Inconceivable Light, Inexpressible Light, Majestic Light, Joyful Light, and Light that Surpasses Sun and Moon.

The impact of light on a person is expressed by Saichi in succinct, everyday language:

> 84,000 delusions,
> 84,000 lights,
> 84,000 joys abounding.

Saichi is filled with delusions—eighty-four thousand, meaning countless—each illuminated and transformed by an equal number of lights. To realize this is to know the endless joy of living.

This imagery of light and its significance was put in contemporary terms by Eikichi Ikeyama, who was a professor of German at Otani University and influenced a whole generation of Shin intellectuals. His poem reads:

The Pure I, which is not-I,
Being in me, reveals to me,
This defiled I.

The Pure I is an aspect of Unhindered Light that illuminates the hidden side of self that is beyond ordinary consciousness. But sooner or later this shadow, the defiled I, is revealed by the working of Light. It is an essential part of oneself. Both the Pure I and defiled I are necessary for a person to attain wholeness. When both are brought to full awareness, we have an awakened, authentic human being.

Once we understand this function of Unhindered Light, we can also appreciate an unusual expression found in Shinran's writings: "deep hearing of the Light." This phrase does make sense, when we realize that Name and Light are synonymous in the sense that both are manifestations of the working of great compassion. Thus, deep hearing of the Name leads to the self being illuminated by Light; and being so illuminated means that one awakens to the Name as fundamental reality. A well-known Shin saying sums up the intimate connection between the two: "The Name is the voiced expression of Light, and the Light is the voiceless expression of the Name."

Unhindered Light not only penetrates the hardest substance in the world, the ego-self, but transforms it into its very opposite, making it soft, supple, and pliable. The transformation comes about because of the compassionate, nurturing warmth of Unhindered Light. It is as natural as ice melting and becoming water. Shinran proclaims:

Having realized true entrusting majestic and boundless
By the working of Unhindered Light,

The ice of blind passion melts without fail
To instantly become the water of enlightenment.

Although the Name (compassionate father) and the Light (compassionate mother) are necessary for religious awakening, they are both outer causes. Only when they work together with the inner cause, faith or *shinjin* as true entrusting, is a new life born. Shinran sums up the relationship of the three:

> Truly we know that without the virtuous Name, our compassionate father, we would lack the direct cause of birth. Without the light, our compassionate mother, we would stand apart from the indirect cause of birth. Although direct and indirect causes may come together, if the karmic-consciousness of shinjin is lacking one will not reach the land of light. The karmic consciousness of true and real shinjin is the inner cause. The Name and light—our father and mother—are the outer cause. When the inner and outer causes are united, one realizes the true body in the fulfilled land.

We now turn to the clarification of true entrusting, or what Shinran calls the "karmic consciousness of shinjin."

FAITH AS TRUE ENTRUSTING

The central experience of Shin Buddhism is called *shinjin*, frequently translated as "faith," but since faith has multiple connotations, it is important to distinguish the different usages of this term. In Buddhism we find three Sanskrit terms that are sometimes translated as "faith." They are *sraddha* (trust), *prasada* (clarity and equanimity), and *adhimukti* (understanding). While shinjin contains some of these elements, Shinran's basic understanding may be best rendered in English as "true entrusting."

In general Buddhism faith frequently comes at the beginning of the religious path, indicating complete trust in the words of the Buddha. Likewise, in Mahayana Buddhism it constitutes the first stage of the religious quest to be followed by the next three stages; thus, faith is followed by understanding, practice, and attainment. In Zen the word faith is often used to denote the total manifestation of absolute selfhood.

Faith is also common in world religions, ranging from the ecstatic *bhakti* in Hinduism to the amazing grace in Protestant Christianity. Faith implies different things for different people: act of will, decision made by reason, way of knowing, overflowing of devotion, gift from God. While the actual experiences may vary, they share a common structure, based on the relationship between the human and divine, the relative and absolute, the sacred and profane.

Shinjin also contains some of these nuances of faith, but central to it is the awakening to reality-as-is, beyond any conceptualized forms of subject-object duality. When Paul Tillich speaks of "the God beyond the God of theism," a comparable Buddhist formulation would be "the Buddha beyond the Buddha of duality." Such a Buddha does not disappear in the direction of transcendence but appears here and now in the midst of everyday life. This movement, described by some as transdescendence, culminates in the appearing of the Name, namu-amida-butsu, in our world.

Shinjin as true entrusting moves in two directions that ultimately become one. On the one hand, a person entrusts the self completely to the Primal Vow, the working of great compassion. And on the other, the person entrusts the self totally to the reality of one's limited karmic self. The latter is made possible by the former. Thus, they constitute a single awakening. This is shinjin or faith as true entrusting.

In daily life mutual trust is the foundation of any kind of meaningful relationship. This is true whether the trust is between individuals, nations, ethnic, social, or religious groups. Without this trust we cannot work together and society cannot function. With this mutual trust, however, we keep promises,

make appointments, observe rules and regulations, and uphold
the law. How well this works depends on our resolve, but it is
also subject to human frailties.

We have all known of promises broken, friendships betrayed,
and treaties abrogated. The whims of self-serving ego tears apart
the web of human relationships, splinters the unity of life, erupts
in anger, hatred, spite, violence, and war. The breaking of trust
is frequently related to the arrogance of power. The classic example is the violation of more than four hundred treaties that
the U.S. government signed with the various Native American
nations. Not a single one was honored.

When I was looking for my first teaching job, various promises were made to me by people only to be broken later. I felt
powerless and angry, because my trust in people had been vio-
lated. I complained about my predicament to one of my Buddhist teachers who knew my situation well. I told him, "I'm
never going to trust another human being!" And he replied, "Of
course not. How can you trust others when you can't even trust
your own self." That not only shut me up but made me question
my own fidelity to the trust others place in me.

If one cannot trust even oneself, if the self is so unreliable,
how can the so-called faith of such a person have any meaning?
Faith in the ordinary sense, based on the unstable ego-self, is not
only unreliable but it is also easily disposable, depending on the
situation. But shinjin emerges from that which is true, real, and
sincere, enabling us to let go of the grasping ego and to entrust
the self to reality that is all sustaining and abiding. This reality is
called by various names: Primal Vow, Immeasurable Light and
Life, Amida Buddha, or simply true and real life.

Faith that originates from the ego-self cannot produce true
spirituality, because it constantly seeks to enhance its life
through wealth, prestige, power, fame, and so on and even uses

religion for its own benefit. When the primary concern is with the utility value of religion, one is vulnerable to cults, superstitious beliefs, sorcery, and magic—anything that serves to inflate the ego-self. This also leads to religious fundamentalism and fanaticism that misuses faith for purposes of self-aggrandizement.

I translate shinjin as not simply entrusting but *true* entrusting to underscore its source as that which is true, real, and sincere—the working of great compassion. Coming as a gift from reality that is true, real, and sincere, and thus not rooted in the unstable ego-self, it can never be broken or shattered. This endowment enables us to naturally entrust ourselves to reality-as-is. When the consequences of karmic life are spent, ultimately true entrusting culminates in supreme enlightenment.

We shall explore more fully the working of the Primal Vow, but for now suffice it to say that true entrusting has a certitude that does not require confirmation or affirmation. Such expression as "I believe" or "I have faith" is superfluous. When the sun is shining brightly in the light of day, who would proclaim, "I believe that the sun is shining"? Or when rain is falling everywhere, what need is there to testify to it, saying, "I have faith that it is raining"?

Shinran frequently uses the expression "ocean of true entrusting." When one enters the vast ocean of Amida's compassion, no longer is there any need to assert the ego-self. One lives naturally and spontaneously within the boundless and fathomless ocean, sustained by the buoyancy of salt water. There is no fear of ever drowning, and all karmic evil will be eventually transformed into ocean water.

This is the reason that while the goal on the Path of Sages is enlightenment, the ultimate goal of Shin Buddhist life is true entrusting. True entrusting inevitably and necessarily leads to supreme enlightenment. Thus, the greatest challenge for us is shinjin or true entrusting. In the words of Shinran:

> For the foolish and ignorant who are ever sinking in birth-and-death, the multitude turning in transmigration, it is not attainment of unexcelled, incomparable fruit of enlightenment that is difficult. The genuine difficulty is true entrusting.

The difficulty of true entrusting is due to self-enclosure, the powerful urge for the ego-self to shield and protect itself. The more it confronts life's difficulties, the more it withdraws into its protective shell. What we must realize is that true entrusting does not depend on what "I" do or what "I" believe; rather, the self opens itself up to the working of true compassion. Or, to put it more precisely, in the words of Saichi:

> My heart is your heart;
> Your heart is my heart.
> It is your heart that becomes me;
> It is not that I become Amida,
> But Amida becomes me—
> Namu-amida-butsu.

The person of true entrusting becomes trustworthy in the most ordinary sense of the word. The reason is that the basis of trust is not the fickle human mind but the abiding reality of Immeasurable Light and Life. Such a person is neither especially good nor virtuous. To be trustworthy is simply the most natural way of living as a true, real human being.

AWAKENING

12

南
無
阿
彌
陀
佛

Awakening is the ultimate goal of the Buddhist path, no matter what school or tradition one may follow. From a narrow, ego-centered world one is awakened to an open, limitless world. In Pure Land vocabulary one realizes the limits of self-power and awakens to the vast universe of Other Power. In the language of Heidegger calculative thinking gives itself up to meditative thinking, a "thinking which is open to its contents, open to what is given."

The highest form of awakening is Buddhahood that has a single clear focus: the deliverance of all beings drowning in the ocean of samsara. This is summed up in the classical East Asian definition of a "Buddha":

> Self-awakening,
> Awakening others;
> Endless the process
> Of the activity of awakening.

Awakening is dynamic, constantly evolving in accordance with life's realities—unfolding from ego-self to compassionate self, from enclosed self to open self, from foolish self to enlightened self.

Several years ago one of my students, Kate, participated in the annual Japan-America Student Conference. Started in 1934, it is a prestigious gathering of the top eighty students from both countries. It holds a four-week traveling seminar during the summer in the U.S. and Japan in alternating years. Kate attended the conference when it was held in Japan. A series of round-table discussions were held in various cities, starting in Tokyo and culminating in Nagasaki in August.

Due to the demanding schedule and the hot, humid weather, Kate was fatigued and restless. When the group came to the Nagasaki Peace Plaza, dedicated to the victims of the 1945 atomic holocaust, they came to a large fountain spraying cool water into the summer heat. When Kate first saw the fountain, she just wanted to jump in, cool her body, and soothe her fatigue. But when she saw the plaque that read "This fountain is dedicated to the children of Nagasaki who died crying for water," such thoughts completely vanished. Instead her thoughts turned to the dying, burned children, the unspeakable horror of war, the inhumanity of humankind that runs deep.

At that very moment Kate experienced a radical awakening, a transformation of consciousness, which completely changed her life. Her thoughts no longer fixated on herself and her needs— they were now directed to the plight of others in need. And this was not a momentary sentimentalism at work. Returning to her college, she concentrated on elevating the status of low-income students and welfare mothers. She eventually graduated from law school as an effective advocate for the poor, the underprivileged, and the disenfranchised.

Many people experience this type of awakening, but normally it touches only one aspect of life and rarely involves the total person. Furthermore, a single experience may not effect any real transformation. The awakening must be repeated and deepened for as long as we are living and breathing. As one writer put it, "It isn't like you have one rite of passage, one death-rebirth experience, and then you Get It!" Hakuin, who revitalized Rinzai Zen in eighteenth-century Japan, spoke of awakening (*satori*) on two stages: initial awakening through use of the koan-riddles, and subsequent series of awakening to deepen the first exposure, the latter being even more important on the path.

Buddhist awakening differs in two ways from ordinary forms of heightened consciousness. First is the somatic involvement, such that the final test of real transformation is a body-mind that has become supple, pliant, and gentle. The somatic emphasis helps us avoid playing mind games and engaging in discursive strategies. Second is the shattering of the conventional notions of I, me, and mine that opens the self up to bottomless and endless reaches of life itself. This is evident in the goals of various Buddhist traditions.

Awakening in Yogacara Buddhism occurs with the turnabout (*paravritti*) at the base of the whole mind-system, deep below our normal consciousness and involving the entire phenomenal world. In Hua-yen Buddhism the enlightenment experience is symbolized by a huge flower garland, *Gandavyuha,* placed on the entire universe, signifying a cosmic awakening. In Pure Land Buddhism the karmic bondage from the beginningless beginning of time is transformed into the very content of supreme awakening, dedicating itself to the salvation of all beings, including a single blade of grass.

TRANSFORMATION

13

南
无
阿
弥
陀
佛

In Shin Buddhism awakening involves the transformation of *bonno* or blind passion into the contents of enlightenment. The term comes from the
Sanskrit *klesha,* but the literal meaning of this Japanese rendition, bonno, is "that which agitates
mind and body." The source of this incessant
agitation is deep-rooted self-centeredness. It is
normally hidden from our sight but becomes ap-
parent when one tries to lead the highest moral
and religious life.

Since our eyes are made to see outwardly, we
criticize others constantly and always blame others for our problems. But if we could reflect even
for a moment, the shortcoming may be our own
and not the other. Through the working of great
compassion that moves in unexpected and unknown ways, we are shown to be frequently pro-
jecting our own defects on others. Unless we be-

come sensitive to this hidden aspect in ourselves, our efforts to change the world will simply contribute to creating greater chaos. The deep insight into the true nature of the ego-self is central to all schools of Buddhism.

Prince Shotoku, who is considered to be the father of Japanese Buddhism, incorporated this insight into his so-called Seventeen-Article Constitution, promulgated in 604 C.E. Although not an official, legal document, he sought to make it the foundation of the newly emerging nation-state of Japan. Article X of his Constitution reads:

> Let us cease from wrath, and refrain from angry looks.
> Nor let us be resentful when others differ from us. For
> all men have heart, and each heart has its own leanings.
> . . . For we are all, one with another, wise and foolish,
> like a ring which has no end. Therefore, although others
> give way to anger, let us on the contrary dread our own
> faults, and although we alone may be in the right, let us
> follow the multitude and act like them.

This is an example of a practical way to deal with self-delusion, incorporating the Buddhist understanding of human nature and the Confucian ideal of social harmony. The latter is summed up in the following words of Confucius: "The superior man seeks harmony, not sameness; the small-minded seeks sameness, not harmony." (*Analects* XIII:23)

The awareness of bonno is especially keen in the Pure Land tradition because the Light of compassion illuminates and focuses on this karmic reality. A contemporary Shin poet expresses this awareness in two poems, using everyday language. The first reads:

Ashamed am I of myself
The darkness
Was my darkness

The circumstances that prompted this poem are unclear, but the poet was obviously agitated about something. Whatever it may have been, he must have blamed the other for what had happened. But in putting forth his best efforts to resolve the situation, it dawned on him that it was due to his own ignorance, not any lacking in the other. This is not self-pity. His admission, "the darkness was my darkness," acknowledges the reality of an imperfect human being.

The second poem suggests that this awakening is not simply a onetime event. The darkness has a long and deep murky past. Thus, it is called *karmic,* so deep that we cannot even fathom the countless lives through which it evolved. And it is *evil,* because the agitation of mind and body creates turmoil and pain for everyone, including oneself. But it is this karmic evil that is the object of great compassion.

Lost and confused have I been
For a long, long time.
While being lost and confused,
I never knew that
I was lost and confused.

Intellectually, it is very difficult to acknowledge one's ignorance, confusion, and failure, but we all experience them in one way or another. And the more we try to deny them, the more persistent their negative effects on our life. Only by acknowledging our karmic evil can we become liberated from it. This is the climax to C. S. Lewis's novel, *Till We Have Faces,* a modern retelling of the legend of Cupid and Psyche.

The principal character in this novel is Orual, the Queen of Glome, who was an unwanted and unloved daughter of the ruling king. She has two sisters who are both more attractive than she. In fact, so great is her ugliness that Orual hides her face behind a veil. But as a queen, Orual is strong-willed, independent, and successful in her own way. Though served selflessly by her ministers, tutor, bodyguard, servants, and others, she is constantly critical of them. She even keeps a notebook of complaints about everyone around her, including her two sisters. At the end of the novel she reads her litany of complaints to the gods.

As she begins to read, rebuking everyone around her, for the first time she hears her own authentic voice speaking: "There was given to me a certainty that this, at last, was my real voice." When she concludes, only silence prevails and there is no response. But suddenly she realizes that "The complaint was the answer. To have heard myself making it was to be answered." All the shortcomings, foibles, and ingratitudes she had ascribed to others were nothing but aspects of her limited self. When she realized this, she came to know herself for the first time.

Orual now had a face. Thus, she could come face to face with the gods. She demonstrates this simultaneous discovery in spiritual awakening. In the words of the medieval Christian mystic Julian of Norwich:

> Our passing life which we have here does not know in our senses what our self is, but we know in our faith. And when we know and see, truly and clearly, what our self is, then we shall truly and clearly see and know our Lord God in the fullness of joy.

In short, Orual was nothing but her complaining self; it was not
a conscious, deliberate choice, but this was her naked reality. She
could neither negate this self nor transcend it. Rather in fully
acknowledging her bonno-nature, her karmic evil, a transformation occurred, enabling her to come face-to-face with the gods.

In Shin Buddhist experience this transformation is brought
about by great compassion. Shinran defined the working of
boundless compassion as *jinen*, a term usually translated as "nature." But this is not nature as objectively understood today that
might be called *natura naturata* (created nature) in contrast to its
dynamic aspect, *natura naturans* (creative nature). Simply put, *jinen*
is "to be made to become so," focusing on the dynamic creativity inherent in each form of life; thus, open to change, growth,
and self-realization. This is the meaning of "virtue" that we
encounter frequently in English translations of Shin works. It
has very little to do with morality but conveys the Greek sense
of "the power of being and the fulfillment of meaning."

Shinran saw in the rhythm of dynamic creativity a transformative power that overcomes the consequences of karmic evil,
no matter how deeply rooted in countless past lives:

> "To be made to become so" means that without the
> practicer's calculation in any way whatsoever, all his
> past, present, and future evil karma is transformed into
> the highest good. To be transformed means that evil
> karma without being nullified and eradicated is made
> into the highest good, just as all river waters, upon en-
> tering the great ocean, immediately become ocean water.

The centripetal self-concern is transformed into centrifugal
other-concern by the power of great compassion without nullifying or eradicating karmic evil. This may sound illogical and

unreasonable, but it is possible because evil in Buddhism has no ontological status.

Transformation on the everyday level is a very common experience. We have all known people who made a virtue out of weakness. A Demosthenes who overcame stuttering to become a master of oratory. An Einstein who flunked mathematics but revolutionized physics with his theory of relativity. An Amy Van Dyken who suffered chronic asthma but won four Gold medals in swimming in the 1996 Atlanta Olympics. When such a positive transformation takes place, the difficulties in life become challenges, rather than obstacles, to fulfilling one's life.

Unlike these examples, however, that involve only one aspect of a person's life, the transformation on the Shin path involves the whole self, both conscious and unconscious, body and mind. According to Shinran's favorite metaphor of ice and water:

> Having gained true entrusting majestic and profound
> By virtue of Amida's Unhindered Light,
> The ice of blind passion melts without fail
> To become the water of enlightenment.

Here several points should be noted. First, the Unhindered Light of Amida illuminates blind passion or bonno, making it clearly evident for the first time. That awareness is brought about by the working of Light. Second, Unhindered Light does not crush blind passion but "melts" it and makes it the very content of enlightenment. The working of great compassion is natural and spontaneous. And third, all this occurs "without fail," due to the Primal Vow that has its own karmic inevitability that no human or divine forces can obstruct. The nature of this transformation is further elucidated:

Evil hindrance becomes the substance of virtue,
As in the case of ice and water.
The more the ice, the more the water.
The more the hindrance, the more the virtue.

The assumption here is that evil hindrance (ice) is not simply dissolved into the virtue of enlightenment (water), once and for all, but that karmic evil continues to produce its effects as long as we are imperfect human beings. This means that contradictory elements are essential for the transformation. That is, evil hindrance is melted to form the content of enlightenment, but at the same time karmic evil, together with its illumination, becomes even more abundant and clear. Such an insight forms the noetic core of true entrusting.

TWO KINDS OF
COMPASSION

14

南無阿彌陀佛

Two kinds of compassion are distinguished in
Tannisho IV: compassion on the Path of Pure
Land, based on the working of Other Power; and
compassion on the Path of Sages, based on self-
power. We first turn to Shinran's description of
the latter path:

> The compassion in the Path of Sages is
> expressed through pity, sympathy, and
> care for all beings, but truly rare is it that
> one can help another as completely as
> one desires.

As human beings, we all feel pity, sympathy, and
care for people in pain and suffering, but how
many of us truly act according to our feelings and
carry out our intention to the very end?

Some years ago I tried to help a young
couple having marriage problems. Being good

friends, I didn't want to see them go through a bitter divorce. So I talked to them together as a couple, then separately several times, attempting to find some areas of reconciliation. Initially, I really felt that I could help them, but as time passed, the situation became increasingly difficult. The same old recriminations were repeated over and over again. They both slowly began to irritate me. The whole affair was taking up too much of my precious time, reconciliation appeared to be impossible, my energy was being spent for nothing.

As this went on for days and weeks, I began to despair: Why am I wasting my time on such knuckleheads? Maybe I shouldn't be attempting amateur marriage counseling? What am I getting out of this? The straw that broke the camel's back was a telephone call from the husband at 2 A.M. one night. Obviously drunk, he wanted to come to my house and talk to me. I told him that it was in the middle of night, so I couldn't see him. He really got upset, so I just cut him off and shouted: "You're an adult, take care of your own damn problems!"

I was much too "conscious of doing good" and probably creating more problems for all three of us. How true the words of Shinran that follow the above quotation:

> In this life no matter how much pity and sympathy we may feel for others, it is impossible to help another as we truly wish; thus our compassion is inconsistent and limited.

But this does not mean abandoning concern for others; rather, it opens up the possibility of true compassion as taught in the Path of Pure Land. In the words of Shinran, "Only the saying of nembutsu manifests the complete and never-ending compassion which is true, real, and sincere." What does this mean? Let us first turn to an example of such a compassion at work.

A story is told about Kichibei, who made his living as a traveling salesman. One day his wife had a stroke and became bedridden, so he was forced to quit his work, stay at home, and take care of his hapless wife. Once, after almost two years had elapsed, a villager remarked to him about how exhausting it must be to care for his wife, day in and day out. Whereupon, Kichibei answered, "No, I never experience fatigue, because every day is both the first experience and the last experience." How are we to understand this answer? What went through his mind as he responded? How could he say that it was not a burden at all? Various possibilities exist.

Kichibei's reply might have come from a complete acceptance of the Buddhist teaching of impermanence. Since time passes from moment to moment, each moment is the first and last experience. When we live every instant of our lives fully, burdens are no longer burdens, for they too shall pass. "Every day is both the first experience and the last experience."

He also could have been manifesting selflessness in which no distinction is made between self and other. Like Vimalakirti of the scripture bearing his name, the illness of another becomes one's own illness. This is complete identification, and no distinction between self and other exists. Hence, taking care of his wife was nothing less than caring for himself.

It is also conceivable that Kichibei's caring might have been based on a very practical reason. Appreciative for all that his wife had done for him throughout their life together, it was only natural that he now looks after her needs. He is motivated by a sense of gratitude that is regarded as central to the ethical and moral life.

As a person of nembutsu, however, Kichibei's response

comes from an entirely different world. Having steeped himself in deep hearing and awakening to the boundless compassion of Amida, he could be himself. Thus, struggling with his wife's condition, he surely must have thought: Why did this happen to me? Why am I so unlucky, compared to my friends? Why doesn't her family come and help? Why can't the doctor do something? I wonder if she'll ever be well again? And in the very pit of despair he must have wished, I hope she would die! But the instant that such self-centered thoughts arose, completely disregarding his wife, the words of Shinran rang in his ears:

> Difficult it is to be free of evil thoughts,
> The heart is like snake and scorpion;
> Good acts, too, are filled with poison,
> They are but deeds empty and vain.

> The appearance of goodness and diligence
> Is for everyone a matter of outward form;
> Because of the abundance of greed, anger
>   and falsehood,
> Deceit and lies fill this self.

Kichibei could express his true sentiments, because he lived within boundless compassion that provided ample space for him to be his truly human self. But having affirmed his karmic reality as a limited, foolish being, he could also identify with his wife's own karmic life that resulted in her illness. She, of course, did not choose to become ill, bedridden, and burdensome; and he, too, did not want to be so self-centered and unfeeling. Yet within boundless compassion Kichibei could affirm his limited karmic reality and also accept his wife's condition as it was. Free of any ego-centered doubting, questioning, and blaming of others, he concentrated on the day-to-day care of his wife with love and devotion.

When I sought to find the one word of compassion to comfort my friend's mother, devastated by the suicide of an only son, I realized that no human word could share in her painful loss and grief. Ordinary words, no matter how eloquent, cannot capture the deep pain and sorrow of any tragic loss. The reason is that indescribable suffering comes from the very source of life itself, inherent in the deep structure of existence. That source is beyond the reach of ordinary language or conventional thinking. But it is from that very depth that the nembutsu, "Namu-amida-butsu" as the healing word, springs forth. Whether vocalized or not, the nembutsu affirms each karma-bound being's reason for living and reason for dying.

The compassion, boundless and endless, ultimately releases us from all self-fixations, carrying our pain and sorrow into a deeper appreciation of life both here and now and into the unknown future. With my friend's mother I could share the universe of namu-amida-butsu: I receive her pain—to the extent that I can; I bear the suffering with her—though never to the same degree. We are both lost, confused and pained, secure in the knowledge of the working of Immeasurable Light and Immeasurable Life.

Shinran's discussion of the two kinds of compassion concludes with the words:

> The compassion in the Pure Land is to quickly attain Buddhahood, saying the nembutsu, and with the true heart of compassion and love save all beings.

The saying of nembutsu as the compassionate expression of Immeasurable Light and Life is the love that embraces my friend

Teruo, his mother, and myself, each a karma-bound being.
When we awaken to this elemental fact, we are all on the path to
Buddhahood. "Quickly attain Buddhahood" connotes the transcendence of conventional diachronic time to enter an entirely
different order of reality.

CONSPIRACY
OF GOOD

15

The ethical life in Buddhism is inseparable from
the religious life. One upholds the ethical as a
necessary basis for religious practice; and it is
also the natural consequence of walking the path
of enlightenment. One always strives to be truly
human in the context of everyday thought,
speech, and action. This means that while Buddhist ethics are based on universal principles,
such as nonviolence and the sacredness of all life,
their application to concrete situations will differ,
depending on the particular circumstances of
each case. This is no simple matter, for example,
in such cases as abortion, for which there is never
a clear-cut answer. Buddhist ethics, however, attempts to maximize personal responsibility and
minimize hypocrisy in dealing with difficult issues.

    The basis for this is the elemental fact of the
interdependence and interconnectedness of all

life. This means that while we may not be capable of always truly and sincerely loving others, we are always the beneficiaries of the concerns, sacrifices, and goodwill of others. In realizing this we will want to serve others and serve society to the best of our ability. Such an understanding of ethical life is expressed in practical terms by the Dalai Lama:

> Since at the beginning and end of our lives we are completely dependent on the kindness of others, how can it be that in the middle we would neglect kindness to others.

In his bestseller, *The Book of Virtues,* William Bennett devotes the second chapter to "Compassion." He includes thirty-five inspirational stories, tales, poems, addresses, and anecdotes by writers as diverse as Aesop, Emily Dickinson, Shakespeare, De Tocqueville, Tolstoy, and Brothers Grimm to encourage the practice of compassion. It comes between the first chapter, "Self-discipline," and the third, "Responsibilities." Bennett thus hopes to encourage readers, especially young people, to be self-reliant, compassionate, and responsible. These qualities are essential for any thinking person but also necessary for the maintenance of social order.

But true compassion is possible only when its real source is known. In order to clarify the source, we begin by asking ourselves: Am I always truly loving? Do I show real, consistent compassion to others? How can I truly be compassionate, especially to spouse, parents, children, and neighbors, especially in their moments of need? Do I, as an adult, possess the right to urge others to practice love and compassion, when I myself am not up to it?

At a Shin Buddhist retreat at Asilomar, California, some

years ago, a young woman shared her insights about an incident regarding her father. She said that she had been incommunicado with him for the last fifteen years, due to a profound misunderstanding. But she recently heard through the grapevine that her father was in a hospital, awaiting a leg amputation. Feeling sorry for him whom she remembered as a vigorous, active man, she decided to visit him at the hospital. But before doing so, she thought that she should first check with her sister and see if it would be all right to see him. After all, she hadn't seen or talked to him for fifteen years. When she telephoned to ask, her sister replied, "Of course, it's all right to visit him. Dad has been calling me, asking about you—about your health, what you're doing, and how you're managing—every week for the last fifteen years."

The young woman was taken aback, completely unaware of her father's compassion directed to her all these years. She had felt only bitterness, anger, and spite. But now she was overcome with a deep sense of shame and remorse for all the aggravations and worries she had created. Deeply grateful to her father's compassion that provided her the boundless space to be her willful self, she planned to see her father immediately after the retreat and make up for the lost time. This awakening restored not only her bond with her father, but she began to relate to others in need, returning to the world the care, concern, and compassion her father had shown her.

An even more impressive story of compassion comes from England. A six-year-old girl went into convulsions, due to a 107-degree temperature, and slipped into a coma. She never regained consciousness and died thirty-seven years later. During that entire time, her father held down three jobs to pay off the medical bills. All of her needs were taken care of by her mother who bathed her every day and prepared a liquid diet four times a day to feed her through tubes. In order to prevent bedsores, she turned her daughter's body at regular intervals. Ultimately the daughter passed away without ever waking up. The parents' love kept her alive for thirty-seven years, but did she ever know the tireless and selfless care that sustained her?

Unlike this young woman, I myself possess full consciousness, the ability to think, and control of all my powers. Yet, I ask myself: Am I aware of all the forces of life that have supported me all these years? Do I fully acknowledge the love that my parents showered upon me? Can I count the number of those who have given of themselves to me, making my life possible? Do I ever think of all the people, both known and unknown, who have made me what I am today? When I take leave of this world, will I do so gratefully, fully aware of all my indebtedness?

I am afraid my answer is not totally positive. I am no different from Joseph K. in Kafka's novel *The Trial*. In the middle of his life, Joseph K. is arrested by the authorities. Throughout the novel he makes repeated attempts to cope with his predicament, figure out the reason for his arrest, and dispose of his case systematically and rationally. A successful bank clerk, he feels that he can deal with the arrest as he deals with his job. But in the end he fails. The novel concludes, "It was as if the shame of it must outlive him." Just as his surname remains incomplete, Joseph K.'s life is incomplete, unfulfilled, and wasted.

Joseph K.'s "arrest" was due to his failure to acknowledge a reality greater than himself that made his life possible. Religiously speaking, it is the lack of sensitivity to boundless compassion that caused his arrest and deprived Joseph K. of a full and rich life. After all, how was he able to survive for nine months in his mother's womb? And taken care of during infancy, receive education from teachers, showered kindness by others, and able to pursue a successful career? Surely it was not by his powers alone. But *The Trial* awaits each of us who may be arrested at any time in the course of our life.

That we may have only a very limited appreciation of life was brought home to me recently in a most unexpected way. We have a pet dog, a Lhasa Apso called Shaypa, which means "Beloved One" in Tibetan. I found a little flyer in her dog food bag that stated: "A dog's sense of smell is about one million times better than yours or mine." One million times! With such a fantastic ability, I thought, Shaypa's world must be infinitely more vast, rich, and interesting than mine. Compared to her, I rely mainly on thinking and my senses for survival, but how limiting and confining that is! Ordinarily this is not an issue, until I encounter an insolvable problem. In trying to resolve it my thinking becomes clouded and my senses totally confused. I lose direction and cannot find a way out of the impasse. According to Buddhism, the turmoil in our life is rooted in dualistic or dichotomous thinking that we never question, but it contains the seeds of our delusions. We will have more to say about this later.

Our karmic ignorance chooses to remain in the darkness of self-enclosure, shutting out the boundless compassion that sustains us. Nevertheless, true compassion works tirelessly on each of us until we attain full awakening. Even at the end of his long and productive life, Shinran continues to express profound gratitude to the ceaseless working of compassion:

> Although my eyes blinded by passions
> Do not see the warm light that embraces me,
> Great compassion never tires
> Constantly casting light upon me.

Critics may charge that compassion as the basis for the ethical life is too subjective and personal to have any impact on society,

yet it is one person, one individual, who can change the course
of history to mitigate human suffering and save many lives. The
legacy of brave individuals who helped save Jewish lives in World
War II is a case in point. This dawned on me when I heard a
public lecture recently at Smith College by Hillel Levine, the
author of the book *In Search of Sugihara*.

The names of Oskar Schindler and Raoul Wallenberg are
very well known, but few have heard of the remarkable deeds of
Chiune Sugihara, a Japanese consul in Kaunus, Lithuania, who
saved the lives of thousands of Jewish refugees in 1940 by issuing transit visas so that they could escape the Nazi persecution.
In the 1930s the policy of the German government was to expel
all Jews from European soil. The Holocaust was to come later.

According to the research by Levine, the U.S. State Depart-
ment, as well as the British Foreign Office, issued orders to its
embassies and consulates in Europe to limit issuing visas to Jews.
The American diplomats stationed in European countries even
went out of their way to discourage Jews from applying for visas.
Sugihara wired his government in Tokyo, requesting permission
to issue transit visas to the Jews, and three times he was turned
down because of its alliance with Germany. Yet he continued to
issue at least six thousand visas even on the train as he left
Kaunas after the Russian occupation. For his heroic act Sugihara
received the Righteous Among Nations Award in 1985 from the
Israeli Holocaust Memorial Yad Vashem.

Levine calls Sugihara's deed a "conspiracy of good," con-
trasting it to the well-known phrase "conspiracy of evil." His act
of compassion created a ripple effect, the foremost example being the fact that immigration officials permitted the Jews to
travel safely through Russia to Japan and other destinations. The
might of government, the power of institutional religion, the

goodwill of philanthropists and the ethically minded failed the Jewish people in World War II, but the efforts of a single person, such as Sugihara, saved the lives not only of the Jews who received visas but their countless offsprings and descendants, an estimated forty thousand lives.

ATTAINMENT WITHOUT A TEACHER

16

The historical Buddha initially studied under various teachers and yogic masters of his time, but ultimately he left them and went off on his own. Meditating under the Bodhi tree, he discovered his own path, the Middle Way, avoiding the extremes of hedonistic pleasures and ascetic self-mortifications. His attainment, thus, is called "attainment without a teacher." Here is the paradigm of Buddhist religious life: the truly awakened person takes refuge in the Buddha Dharma and does not rely on a teacher, another karma-bound being. This fact is central to the diverse paths of Buddha Dharma, including that of Pure Land.

This, of course, does not mean that we should not receive guidance from mature, experienced teachers. The prototype of a true seeker, the youth Sudhana in the *Gandavyuha*, makes a pilgrimage to fifty-three teachers of diverse backgrounds, both laity and renunciants. But it does mean that in the final attainment of liberation, autonomous selfhood, embodying dharma, is born. This is explicit, for example, in the final sermon of the Buddha, when he exhorts his disciples, "Be ye lamps unto yourselves. Rely on yourselves, and do not rely on external help. Hold fast to the truth as a lamp and seek salvation in the truth alone, looking not for assistance to anyone besides yourselves." The key word here is "truth" or dharma. The reliance is not upon the fragile ego-self but upon the dharma fully manifested. This results in the awakening of an autonomous self that is the goal of the Buddhist path.

Wisdom and compassion always work together as the two wings of a bird or the two wheels of a cart, but their functions differ. In Shin Buddhism the compassion of the Buddha encapsulated in the Primal Vow focuses on each person. This compassionate activity endows wisdom in a person, and this endowment makes one autonomous and independent. Perhaps this can be illustrated by a concrete example. The educational philosophy of a certain school for the physically challenged in Kyoto aims to make each student strong and self-reliant.

If a child is learning to walk in spite of weak, undeveloped legs for whatever reason, the teacher walks right beside her without giving any assistance. If she falls, the teacher falls. Instead of picking up the fallen child, the teacher struggles with all his might to get up. The child copies the teacher, and after many attempts she stands up on her own powers. This is done repeatedly until the child begins to walk by herself.

One teacher was in charge of a thalidomide child who could not eat by himself, having been born without arms. When the lunch period came, he would run and sit next to the teacher, awaiting to be fed. The teacher tried to think of ways to teach him to eat by himself. She wanted him to become independent and not rely on others, but she didn't know what to do. One day on the way home from school she saw a dog lapping food from its bowl. The next day, when the child came running to her side at lunchtime, she said, "Today, you eat by yourself!" She demonstrated by lapping food from the dish in front of her. The child hesitated but eventually copied the teacher. He bent down and lapped his food. Excited and delighted that he could eat all by himself, he ran home and told his mother.

The following day the boy's mother came to the school, fuming with anger. She was very upset that he had been treated as if he were a dog. She berated the teacher. But upon learning that it was for the good of her son, she, too, went home and ate by lapping her food, as she was told to do. Soon the boy took greater interest in his schoolwork, joined his classmates on the playground, and made friends for the first time. These stories remind us that true compassion is not simply a matter of the heart; it must find ways to affirm the independence of each person.

Simone Weil, one of the few Western writers familiar with the Pure Land teaching during her lifetime, writes about compassion in her book *Waiting for God*. She spoke from the standpoint of a worker, having spent time in an automobile factory in France.

> Those who are unhappy have no need for anything in this world but people capable of giving them their attention. The capacity to give one's attention to a sufferer is a very rare and difficult thing; it is almost a miracle; it is a miracle. Nearly all those who think they have this capacity do not possess it. Warmth of heart, impulsiveness, pity are not enough.

Attention here means to attend to the needs of the other not from a privileged, superior position but from the standpoint of the other as a human being. This, of course, requires tremendous wisdom since one must find ways to enable the other to develop a sense of selfhood with integrity. The ability to do so is true compassion, which is wisdom in action.

Such a way of thinking, affirming the autonomy of each person, lies in the background of Shinran's pronouncement in *Tannisho* VI: "As for myself, Shinran, I do not have a single disciple. If I could make others say the nembutsu through my own devices, they would be my disciples. But how arrogant to claim as disciples those who live the nembutsu through the sole working of Amida's compassion."

Historically, Shinran had a large following during his years in the Kanto district, following his exile and far away from the capital, but he did not want people to depend upon him as a teacher. The sole working of Amida's compassion, embodied in the life of a karmic being, ensures independence and self-reliance. Rooted in boundless compassion, such a self is not the small-minded ego, but the person who has realized autonomy interrelated and interconnected with all of existence.

HUMILITY

17

The Sanskrit term for a good friend, *kalyanamitra*, connotes something more than just a friend; it suggests someone (or something) that becomes a guide, a teacher, and an inspiration on a person's journey on the path of enlightenment. Even difficult circumstances can serve this purpose. Illness can be such a friend, for it teaches us humility and gratitude. The full awareness of human finitude, fragility, and mortality should naturally make us humble. But it is impossible to become humble on our own, for if we think we have succeeded, at that very instant we become prideful and arrogant.

In East Asia the practice of humility is encoded in social behavior, especially in the etiquette of bowing. To bow one's head is to humble oneself, the direct opposite of asserting the ego-self. Bowing is especially important when entering a "dojo," a spiritual training center, whether it be a temple, meditation hall, or martial arts class. The significance of bowing is expanded by Shunryu Suzuki, the pioneer Zen teacher in America:

> Bowing is a very serious practice. You should be prepared to bow, even in your last moment. Even though it is impossible to get rid of our self-centered desires, we have to do it. Our true nature wants us to. . . . Sometimes the disciple bows to the master, sometimes the master bows to the disciple. A master who cannot bow to his disciple cannot bow to the Buddha. Sometimes the master and the disciple bow together to the Buddha. Sometimes we may bow to cats and dogs.

An exemplary figure in this vein is the Bodhisattva Never Disparaging in the *Lotus Sutra,* the most popular Buddhist scripture in the whole of East Asia. This bodhisattva constantly bowed with palms together in the act known as *gassho* before anyone he encountered, for he recognized the potential for enlightenment in all beings. Bowing to all people without discrimination was his religious practice.

In the nembutsu, *namu* bows to *amida-butsu,* but not only to Amida, for one bows to all things, great and small. And this expression of humility and gratitude begins in the home, as myokonin Ichitaro once said: *"Namu* means that one's head bows down to all people. Your head bows down also to your wife and children whom you've held under your thumb up to now." As deep hearing transforms the ego-self to an open self, bowing becomes a natural expression of true and real life that flows through a person.

The Japanese expression of grace before meals is *"itadaki-*

masu," said with head bowed and palms placed together. Although today it may be a mere formality, the original intention was to express appreciation for a meal, saying to the food placed before one, "Thank you for giving up your life, so that my own life can be extended." We thank the life of vegetables and plants, of fish and fowl, of animals and other living things. They give up their life, so that we can extend our human life. Cecilia Kapua Lindo sums up this sentiment in "Grateful to All Beings":

From time to time
I too am misled by the myth
That exalts the independent, self-made man.

Upon hearing the voice of the Enlightened One,
Any air of self-importance
Is deflated, like an empty balloon.

And I become aware that my existence depends
Upon the many lives that are slain for me
Each time I sit down to eat my meal.

Here is the realization that human beings cannot live without violating other forms of life. Within this realization is the sorrow of a limited karma-bound being who cannot otherwise survive. There is a universe of difference between believing that humans have the right to take other forms of life with impunity and having to do so with a deep sense of shame, regret, and repentance. The least a person can do, then, is to be grateful and not waste nature's gifts. When we see that human beings do not occupy a special, privileged place in the web of life, then humility and gratitude should be natural and spontaneous. Yet the difficulty in arriving at this understanding is immense.

The finite nature of human existence is a fact of life. We are limited and restricted physically, intellectually, and emotionally. We cannot fly and soar into the sky like a bird, nor can we swim and stay underwater like a fish. No matter how brilliant one may be, a person cannot fathom another's inner feelings, not even those of loved ones. No one really knows anything about life after death in spite of countless speculations. We find it difficult to control jealousy, anger, self-doubt, insecurity, and fear, even though we realize that they are self-defeating. We aspire to be always loving, but in reality we are inconsistent and undependable. The more we aspire to live an exemplary life, ethically and religiously, the more we are made aware of our karmic limitations.

While Confucius is revered as a model teacher who not only taught but lived an ethical life, he himself was the first to acknowledge his limitations. His humility comes through in his admission: "The superior man is ashamed that his words exceed his deeds. . . . The way of the superior man is threefold, but *I have not been able to attain it.* The man of wisdom has no perplexities; the man of humanity has no worries; the man of courage has no fear." (*Analects* 14:30–31) In brief, he admits his lack of wisdom, humanity, and courage, a sign of his greatness as a teacher of humanity.

When we realize that we are all sustained by both visible and invisible forces in our world, we should be humble and grateful. But the reality of human nature is that our karmic impulse goes against both humility and gratitude. To acknowledge this truly is to experience the sadness and sorrow of what it

means to be human. But deeper and profounder than our feelings is the heart of great compassion that takes us in. The
Primal Vow ultimately transforms the hopelessly self-centered
and arrogant person into one who manifests true humility and
gratitude.

ARROGANCE

18

南無阿彌陀佛

While humility is the natural and spontaneous expression of an awakened person, our innate tendency as foolish beings is the very opposite—arrogance that appears in various subtle forms. Buddhists have paid great attention to this fact, for it is a perennial problem and upsets the equilibrium of life. Buddhist literature speaks of seven types of arrogance: common arrogance (*mana*), great arrogance (*adhimana*), multiple arrogance (*manatimana*), arrogance of believing in enduring selfhood (*asmimana*), vain arrogance (*abhimana*), humble arrogance (*unamana*), and deceitful arrogance (*mithyamana*).

The first, "common arrogance," is to feel superior to someone who is clearly inferior in ability, talent, intelligence, appearance, status, and so on. This happens, for example, when we see the homeless wandering in our cities. We feel clearly superior to them. Yet if we should feel pity but do nothing, it is another disguised form of arrogance. But this common arrogance also occurs when we think that we are better than someone of equal status or achievement.

"Great arrogance" is to think that one is better than an equal, but it also includes the notion that one is just as good as someone clearly superior. We find this frequently when we identify ourselves with the best and brightest in a group to which we belong. It can be family, class, race, creed, or nation; sometimes a sports team, social club, college fraternity, business firm, and so on. We act as if we are better than others not because of our individual worth but because of identification with a recognized group.

"Multiple arrogance" or literally "arrogance piled on arrogance" is to feel superior to someone who has everything—money, status, looks, talent, popularity, and influence. This is done by claiming some special knowledge or unique possession, however trivial it may be, that the superior person may lack. We find this in academic one-upmanship among scholars who pride themselves in the knowledge of trifling minutiae.

We are all subject to these three types of arrogance, and very few of us are immune to them. I have a friend, for example, who suffered several heart attacks, requiring a bypass operation each time. The condition of his heart is so poor that doctors have refused further operations. But he dislikes talking about it, because once he mentions it in public, there is always someone who tries to show him up. "Oh, you've had a heart attack; I've had two." "Oh yeah, yours was a triple bypass; I had a quadruple bypass!" "Is that right, you almost died. Well, I was dead . . . until the doctor revived me." And so it goes on and on. This reminds me of the story of Christian desert fathers who were trying to outdo themselves in self-mortification, "dying unto oneself." A monk brags to another, saying, "I'm deader than you are."

The remaining four types are other forms of arrogance that are not usually recognized as such. "Arrogance of enduring selfhood" refers to the unquestioned belief in the existence of a substantial "I." Buddhism teaches the error of grasping the five aggregates (*skandha*) as constituting an enduring selfhood: form (body), sensation, perception, psychic disposition, and consciousness. Although Western philosophers as diverse as Hume, Kant, Nietzsche, and William James have shown the nonexistence of a substantial self, it plays an unquestioned role in our daily life. As long as we assume that such a fictive self is real and enduring, we are the epitome of arrogance.

The negation of the conventional self does not mean that we should not organize our life and make plans for the future. Rather, it urges us to be fully aware of the fleeting nature of existence and not place our whole being on such an undependable self. Buddhists live with such an understanding, as exemplified by Genza, who once said, "As long as man lives, he must work and plan for a thousand years. Even this Genza plants persimmon and chestnut trees. I have lots of work to do in this world. But we must listen to the teaching, as if there's no tomorrow."

"Vain arrogance" is to make false claims about attainment, especially of some kind of spirituality. In the first place true attainment is not possible within conventional thinking, based on the subject-object dichotomy, which inevitably objectifies everything and prohibits self-knowledge. Moreover, if one has realized true attainment, there is no need to talk about it, since all dichotomies have been transcended. There are variations to the following story, but once there was a young samurai who begged to study with a master to perfect the art of swordsmanship. In the interview, he asked how long it would take to perfect the art by practicing hard two hours every day. The master replied, "Four years." Then he asked about practicing four hours every day, and the reply was "Eight years." But when he asked how long it would take to become a master himself, practicing eight hours a day, the answer was "Never!" True mastery of any art is endless, involving both bodily and mental training. Hence, the motto of Noh actors, "Always keep the beginner's mind."

"Humble arrogance" is encountered when people feign humility to attract attention and gain some kind of recognition. There are people who seek sympathy and pity from others to bolster their self-image. Both Christianity and Buddhism teach the virtue of meekness and humility on the religious path. But when this is claimed apart from the truly religious life, it is just another way of seeking special attention.

"Deceitful arrogance" is to inflate oneself by bragging, speaking half-truths, and engaging in double talk. This is, of course, ego-assertion and self-aggrandizement in their most blatant forms. The religious person is fully aware of this potential in one's own being, so the critical eye is turned inward, although our common tendency is to point fingers at others.

We all desire to overcome these forms of arrogance, but the more we try, the more we realize its immense difficulty. The least we can do is to be realistic, admitting our inability to be completely free of them. But this admission is also very, very painful. In fact, this inability is another evidence of a limited karmic being. Genza (1842–1930) was well known for counseling people on Shin faith. Once a man said to him: "I'm a hypocrite. When I go to the temple, I sit in front of Amida and enjoy saying the nembutsu, but when I go home, I forget everything completely. I'm a hypocrite." Thereupon, Genza replied, "But if you admit that you're a hypocrite, that's good, because it's really hard to be a real hypocrite."

TRUE DISCIPLE
OF BUDDHA

19

A contemporary definition of Christian faith was
formulated by Paul Tillich in the following
words: "To accept the acceptance of the unacceptable." The unacceptable is the person of sin,
alienated from self, world, and God. But it is
precisely this sinner who is accepted by Jesus
Christ; he sacrifices his life on the cross for the
sake of the sinner. "Those who are well have no
need for a physician, but those who are sick; I
came not to call the righteous, but sinners."
(Mark 2:17) Faith is the act of accepting this
acceptance by God of the unacceptable sinner.

The discerning reader must have sensed a
similar structure in Shinran's religious thought.
To make this point explicit I shall turn to his
major work, *The True Teaching, Practice, and Realization
of the Pure Land Way*. In the section entitled "True
Disciple of the Buddha," Shinran lists all the
ideal qualities of a true disciple that he culled

from Buddhist literature. Logical thinking would conclude that these qualities would make a person "acceptable" in the eyes of Buddha, but for Shinran that is not the case. Before explaining the reason for this, let us look what the tradition enumerates as some characteristics of an ideal disciple.

- A supple body and mind, unlike the rigid stance and inflexible mind of an arrogant person
- A body and mind filled with peaceful bliss, having been touched by the light of compassion
- A person who manifests great joy in the Dharma and worthy of being a good companion of the Buddha
- A disciple shows clarity of wisdom and excellence of virtues, vast and profound understanding, and majestic virtues
- A person described as a white lotus among people, a king among physicians who cures illness and ensures good health, one revered by all the Buddhas and liberated from the endless cycle of samsara
- A person who manifests great compassion, gains entry into the land of the Buddhas, shows gratitude to Buddha by guiding others into the path of enlightenment, and ascends the ten bodhisattva stages
- A true disciple is embraced and protected by the Buddha, never to be abandoned, and has insight into the nonorigination of all things
- A disciple is praised as the "most excellent among people, the wondrous, excellent person, the best among the best, the rare person, the very finest person" and protected by Avalokitesvara and Mahasthamaprapta

- A person of highest awakening, identical with Maitreya Bodhisattva, receives prediction of supreme enlightenment, and equals Queen Vaidehi to attain joy, awakening, and radiance.

The list concludes with eight historical figures who aspired for the Pure Land as exemplary models among the true disciples of Buddha. Having listed these glowing descriptions, there follows Shinran's deep, painful lament in having fallen far short of the ideal:

I know truly how grievous it is that I, Gutoku Shinran, am sinking in an immense ocean of desires and attachments and am lost in the vast mountain of fame and advantage; so that I rejoice not at all at entering the stage of the truly settled and feel no happiness at coming nearer the realization of true enlightenment. How ugly it is! How wretched it is!

This penetrating self-appraisal is reinforced by the three kinds of people who are difficult to save that he finds in *Mahaparinirvana-sutra*. They are those who slander the Mahayana teachings, those who commit the five transgressions, and those who lack the seeds of Buddhahood, called *icchantika*. Here again instead of seeing others, Shinran finds himself accurately portrayed.

Shinran clearly is unacceptable in the eyes of traditional Buddhism and in his own reflection, for even in his advanced years he is "sinking in the immense ocean of desires and attachments and lost in the vast mountains of fame and advantage." But it is the unacceptable, the being of karmic evil, that is the very focus of the Primal Vow, accepted by the all-embracing, nonexclusive compassion of Amida Buddha. This realization results in Shinran's exultation of joy and gratitude:

> Now, as I ride on the ship of the great compassionate vow and sail on the expansive ocean of wondrous light, the breeze of highest virtue blows peacefully and calms the waves of pain and sorrow. Quickly shall I reach the land of Immeasurable Light and attain unexcelled nirvana.

Tillich's interpretation and Shinran's understanding come from different historical traditions, cultural contexts, and personal experiences, so obviously they are not one and the same. Yet the parallel structure of the relationship of a relative, finite being to a transcendent, infinite reality is striking. This fact alone attests to the validity of religious truths for all ages.

MYOKONIN

20

南無阿彌陀佛

The exemplary practitioners of nembutsu—
Saichi, Kichibei, Ichitaro, Genza, and others—are
called myokonin. This term literally translates as
a "rare good person." It is derived from the Chinese translation of the Sanskrit *pundarika,* lotus
flower, which symbolizes enlightenment. In the
premodern period, they were normally from the
lower classes of Japanese society, usually with
very little formal education. In the earliest standard collection of myokonin stories, compiled in
the nineteenth century, there are accounts of 64
peasants and 28 merchants among the approximately 140 recorded. For example, Genza was a
peasant, although he seems to have owned some
land; Kichibei was a peddler; and Saichi was originally a carpenter who later became a maker of
geta or wooden clogs.

Just as the lotus blooms in muddy water, so
the "rare and good person" blossoms in the muck

and mire of society, brimful with greed, hatred, and foolishness. The lotus of enlightenment will not take root on the high plateaus of abstraction, nor in the rarefied atmosphere of the cloistered retreats. It grows in the swamp of everyday living, filled with crying babies, unpaid debts, noisy neighbors, petty rivalries, and unreasonable bosses. Myokonin were basically lay people, men and women, who labored for a living, had no means to attend extended religious retreats, and could not read the difficult scriptures. Yet, being human like anyone else, they sought answers to the questions regarding living and dying. Guided by nameless teachers, both priests and laity, they came to appreciate the Buddha Dharma that awakened them to the significance of this unrepeatable life.

The standard reading at the beginning of a Buddhist religious service repeats the Three Gems or Jewels—taking refuge in the Buddha, Dharma, and Sangha. It is prefaced by the following statement:

> Hard is it to be born into human life,
>   now we are living it.
> Difficult is it to hear the teaching of the Buddha,
>   now we hear it.

The first line makes little sense until we realize the critical implication of the second line. When we are awakened by the Buddha's teaching to become truly human, we realize for the first time how fortunate we are to be given this life. Born as human beings we are given the opportunity to become liberated from the infinite finitude of samsara. Myokonin, regardless of the station in life, exemplify such a person in Shin Buddhism.

Myokonin are not of a single type. Some are wise and profound in their foolishness; others witty and humorous in self-

effacing ways. Some are energetic and active in society; others
reflective and reclusive. Some are obedient and submissive; others
critical and rebellious. They manifest their respective karmic
potentials, negating any simple stereotyping.

That each person is unique and different accords with the
basic standpoint of Mahayana Buddhism that affirms multiple
realities. A famous Zen koan makes this point explicit: "The ten
thousand things return to the One; to where does the One
return?" The One, of course, returns to and appears in countless
phenomenal particulars that blossom in the realm of awakening.

The rare and good person is not enlightened or virtuous or
saintly in the ordinary sense. Rather, he or she simply affirms
the boundless compassion within which one's limited karmic
self attains full awakening. Such a person thrives within the
openness and love provided by great compassion. In this boundless space a person lives out the effects of past karma but never
again sows the seeds of future suffering. The common denomi-
nator of all myokonin, in spite of their great variety and differences, is a profound sense of thankfulness.

> How grateful!
> When I think of it, all is by Amida's grace.
> O Saichi, what do you mean by it?
> Ah yes, his grace is a real fact.
> This Saichi was made by his grace.
> The clothes I wear,
> The food I eat,
> The footgear I put on.
> Every other thing we have in this world is made
>   by Amida's compassion.
> Including the bowl and the chopsticks.

Even the workshop where I work making
    wooden clogs.
There is really nothing that is not the
    "Namu-amida-butsu."
How happy I am for all this!

But this is not piety in the ordinary sense, and gratitude cannot be fabricated. Saichi demolishes any notion of gratitude preached in doctrinal or ideological language.

To be grateful is not *anjin* (faith confirmed)
Nothing happening is nothing happening.
To be grateful is a fraud—
'Tis true, 'tis true.

LOTUS BLOOMS
IN FIRE

21

"The lotus blooms in fire" is a famous saying from the *Vimalakirti Sutra*, which is quoted throughout East Asia. Fire is the most appropriate symbol for our passions, whether ignited in moments of anger, hatred, and jealousy, or smoldering in agitation, frustration, and insecurity, or overwhelming a person with fear, meaninglessness, and death. But it is in the very midst of these passions that the awakening to new life, the blossoming of lotus flower, occurs. The following incident almost destroyed a Japanese-Argentine family in Buenos Aires, but it is happening everywhere all the time among all kinds of people.

I met Mrs. Tomoda in Kyoto in the summer of 1981, while staying at the Hongwanji International Center. She was from Argentina, spending the summer with her husband, a successful businessman, listening to Shin lectures and talks at various temples. One evening Mrs. Tomoda re-

lated her life story to me, explaining the reason for her presence
in Kyoto far, far away from her home.

She was born in Japan and immigrated to Argentina immediately after World War II. When she was a child in Japan,
Christian missionaries came to her village with food in one hand
and a Bible in the other. She converted to Christianity and
moved to Argentina where she married her present husband.
They had one child, a son, who was now in his early thirties and
involved in the family business. A prosperous, thriving family,
they were active in the local Christian church. Her son even
served as a deacon of the church. One day, however, Mrs.
Tomoda's life was shattered unexpectedly—their son brought
home a white Argentine woman, announcing his intention to
marry her. This went against everything that she had planned for
all her life: a nice Japanese daughter-in-law who would care for
her in old age. She was strongly against any interracial marriage.
It would destroy all her dreams.

Thus began two years of hellish existence, mother and son
bickering and fighting over every little thing. Soon Mrs. Tomoda
began to doubt her faith, for she was not living up to the biblical
injunction of loving one's enemy. She couldn't even love her own
son, let alone an intruder that he had brought home. Then she
vaguely recalled some Shin Buddhist sermons that she had heard
long ago when very young. She especially remembered the stories
about the unconditional, all-embracing love of Amida directed
specifically to foolish beings, consumed with anger and ignorance.

There were no Buddhist temples in Buenos Aires at that
time, so she ordered Shin books and journals from Japan. She
devoured them in desperation. The more she read, the more she
realized that her only path was the nembutsu that assured total
liberation from suffering created by her own ignorance and fool-

ishness. Her feelings were buoyed on reading Shinran's pronouncement: "When we entrust ourselves to Amida's Primal
Vow, we who are like bits of rubble are transmuted into gold."
She realized that it was not her son or his girlfriend who should
be blamed; rather she was the worthless one, useless as bits of
rubble, for whom the path of nembutsu had been readied all
along.

As Mrs. Tomoda began finding her religious roots, it so
happened that the Monshu, the supreme head of the Hongwanji
branch of Shin Buddhism in Kyoto, was visiting Brazil and made
a one-day side trip to Buenos Aires. She went to hear him speak
at a private residence, sitting in a chair at the back of the living
room. Some kind of ritual was being performed, the purpose of
which she did not understand. What she later discovered was
that she had undergone the ceremony of confirmation as a Shin
Buddhist.

When she returned home, Mrs. Tomoda immediately apologized to her son for her willfulness, selfish behavior, and harsh
words. And she gave her blessing to her son to marry the woman
of his choice. She also informed him of her need to return to
her original Shin faith, but that he should continue to serve his
church as he had all these years.

When the mother apologized, the son also responded with
apologies, asking for her forgiveness. He, too, had been stubborn
and rebellious. Soon the two became closer than ever, understanding and appreciative of each other. Each would go his or
her own way with the blessing and support of the other. It was
her son who urged her to go to Japan to immerse herself in deep
hearing of the Buddha Dharma. He would pay for all the necessary expenses.

Mrs. Tomoda's awakening is the lotus blooming in fire. Anger, hatred, and spitefulness that burned within revealed her

reality as a karma-bound being—limited, imperfect, and foolish. But rather than condemning or punishing her, great compassion provides the space to see herself as she is. As she gained insight into herself, Mrs. Tomoda could openly admit her erroneous ways naturally and spontaneously. She thus opens her heart, ashamed and humbled, to her son who, in turn, opens up to her. In this heart-to-heart communication we see the full flowering of humanity, beyond the conventional divisions that are nothing but human constructs. Transcendence of religious, ethnic, gender, and class discriminations is essential in any age, but it is especially so today when our world is being pulled apart by countless divisions.

OCEAN OF THE
PRIMAL VOW

22

One of Shinran's favorite metaphors for the religious life is "entering the ocean of the Primal Vow." The saving vow of Great Compassion is likened to the vast ocean for its all-embracing openness, fathomless depth, and miraculous power to transform everything and make it a part of itself. Thus, the ocean metaphor expresses the compassionate working of Amida Buddha summed up in the phrase "transforming evil into good without nullifying evil."

When Shinran was exiled in 1207 from the capital of Kyoto to the remote district of Echigo in northwestern Japan, he came into intimate contact with the ocean for the first time. But this ocean, today called the Japan Sea, manifested two opposing phenomena depending on the season. In winter the Siberian blasts cause roaring, turbulent waves, but in springtime the same ocean undulates with calm serenity. Shinran must have been deeply impressed by the vitality of nature, evident in both the storm-tossed sea and the peaceful, still ocean.

Resorting to the ocean imagery, Shinran describes the unenlightened life of samsara in vivid metaphors. He speaks of the ocean of sentient beings, ocean of painful birth-and-death, ocean of insatiable desires, vast ocean of human suffering, ocean of deluded passion, ocean of karmic bondage, and the ocean difficult to cross over. But the same ocean is also celebrated in glowing terms: ocean of wisdom, ocean of inconceivable virtues, ocean of the Primal Vow, ocean of Amida's compassion, ocean of great treasures, and limitless ocean of boundless light.

While the two kinds of ocean thus depicted are completely different on the surface, they are in fact one and the same. Here again we see the nondual relationship between samsara and nirvana, deluded passions and enlightenment. Nonduality means that from the deluded viewpoint of samsara it is distinct from nirvana, but from the all-embracing standpoint of nirvana the two are one. In fact, samsara as an essential component of nirvana undergoes transformation into its very opposite by the dynamic working of compassion.

This transformation is a profoundly spiritual happening, centered on the being of karmic evil. Shinran describes this as follows in his *Hymns of the Pure Land Masters:*

> The ocean of the inconceivable Name does not retain
> Even the corpses of evildoers and Dharma-abusers.
> All the rivers of evil entering the ocean
> Become one in taste with the water of virtue.

The evildoers are those who are guilty of the five transgressions, and Dharma-abusers are those who commit blasphemy against the teaching. Such people are considered to be "corpses"—the spiritually dead for whom enlightenment is an impossibility. But they are never forsaken, for the ocean of compassion eventually embraces them and transforms them into beings of enlightenment.

Shinran states that "People who look down on teachers and who speak ill of masters commit slander of the dharma. Those who speak ill of their parents are guilty of the five grave transgressions." If this disqualifies us from the path of enlightenment, who among us is not already a "corpse"? How many of us can say that we have never criticized our teachers, or that we have never talked back to our parents? In spite of this, however, we are all transformed to become "one in taste with the water of virtue." When embraced by the ocean of great compassion, all people, even the most hopeless, will achieve supreme enlightenment.

Regardless of our karmic histories, we will all be taken in by the ocean of the Primal Vow. This, of course, includes my friend who took his own life but now is part of the vast ocean of great compassion. No matter the short span of our destinies on this earth, the boundless compassion of Amida welcomes us and transforms our life into that of unexcelled, supreme enlightenment that is timeless.

> When the many rivers of evil passion enter
> Into the ocean of the Great Compassionate Vow
> Of Unhindered Light, illuminating the ten quarters,
> They become one in taste with the water of wisdom.

ONE BRIGHT PEARL

23

Dogen, the great Zen teacher and contemporary of Shinran, wrote an essay entitled "One Bright Pearl." It articulates the basic standpoint of Mahayana Buddhism, the nonduality of samsara and nirvana, in his inimitable style. Its message parallels the thought of Saichi, who wrote:

> I take delight in this world of delusion,
> For it is the seed of true awakening,
> Taken in by Amida's compassion.
> Namu-amida-butsu, namu-amida-butsu.

While the language of Zen and Shin are naturally different, here we see a similar structure of enlightened reality affirming karmic finitude.

One bright pearl, coined by T'ang master Hsuan-sha, is symbolic of enlightenment.

Once, a monk asked him, "I hear you have said all the universe is one bright

pearl. How can I gain an understanding of that?" The
master said, "All the universe is one bright pearl. What
need is there to understand it?"

The monk's question comes from a dualistic perspective that is
seeking an objective answer. Hsuan-sha's reply comes from a
nondualistic mode, negating any conceptualized notions about
the one bright pearl. He points to true understanding as the
embodying of the one bright pearl. Since it is embodied, there is no
need to "understand" in the conventional sense.

The next day the master himself asked the monk, "All
the universe is one bright pearl. What is your understanding of it." The monk answered, "All the universe is
one bright pearl. What need is there to understand it?"
"I know now," replied Hsuan-sha, "that you are living in
the Black Mountain's Cave of Demons."

In this second exchange, the roles are reversed. The master asks
the monk the same question, as if testing him. But this time the
monk replies from a nondualistic stance. He has come to fully
embody the one bright pearl in his own being. Hsuan-sha's final
comment approves the monk's answer that affirms delusion as
part of the one bright pearl. Delusion is symbolized by the Black
Mountain (the massive darkness of ignorance) and the Cave of
Demons (egoistic self-enclosure).

The main thrust of this exchange—that enlightenment affirms delusion—is made even more explicit later, when Dogen
resorts to another metaphor:

When you are drunk, there is a close friend who will
give the pearl to you, and you, without fail, must impart

the pearl to a close friend. When the pearl is attached to someone, he is, without exception, drunk. It being thus, it is the one bright pearl—all the universe.

Awakening involving the total self contains the reality of drunkenness (delusion) that makes the latter powerless. If this affirmation is lacking, one bright pearl becomes an empty metaphor. It is no different from "flowers blooming in mid-air" or "hairs growing on the shell of a tortoise."

The conclusion to this brilliant essay reiterates the nonduality of enlightenment and delusion: "Even if there is perplexed or troubled thinking, it is not apart from the bright pearl. It is not a deed or thought produced by something that is not the bright pearl. Therefore, coming and going in the Black Mountain's Cave of Demons are themselves nothing but the one bright pearl." True awakening is the realization of our reality as limited karmic beings, brought to awareness by great compassion. This is reality. Thus, "our perplexed or troubled thinking" as karma-bound beings is essential to the one bright pearl.

In Saichi's case Amida's compassion embraces his delusions, transforming them into the source of awakening without nullifying them. As long as we live out our human life on this earth, delusions will continue to appear as the consequence of our karmic past, but we will no longer create further delusions to bring endless, unnecessary suffering to self and others.

24

THE CRY OF CICADAS

南無阿彌陀佛

Japanese poetry reached its apex in the seventeen-syllable haiku of Basho (1644–94), who was a poet and thinker of the first rank. Creating a semantic field with a minimum of words and a preference for nouns, he created space for the imagination to soar and insight to penetrate all things. One of his famous poems in his *Narrow Road to the Deep North* illustrates his dual journey, exploration into northern Japan and into his dark interior:

> Such stillness—
> The cry of cicadas
> Sinks into the rocks.

This haiku evokes memories of a lazy summer afternoon, hot and humid. Unexpectedly, the shrill cry of cicadas, very common in Japan, pierces the stillness. The cry accentuates the silence, but it also penetrates the rocks. How can mere sound sink into hard substance? It doesn't make sense, it's inconceivable, it's ridiculous. So I think, until I see that Basho is describing something more than mere objective phenomenon. He points to a happening taking place at the deepest level of life, unifying the cry, the rocks, the poet, and the universe into a singular experience.

A Shin Buddhist may liken the cry of cicadas to the call of true compassion. The call penetrates the hardest substance in the world: my ego-shell. The Sanskrit term for compassion, *karuna*, contains the root term implying painful moaning or groaning, arising from the identification with the pain and suffering in the world. This was the inspiration of the Primal Vow, awakened by Dharmakara Bodhisattva, out of profound sorrow for beings drowning themselves in the ocean of samsara. It took ten immense kalpas of galactic time to fulfill the Vow to save all beings and qualify for supreme enlightenment. Having fulfilled it and becoming Amida Buddha, all beings without a single exception will be liberated from the throbbing afflictions of body and mind.

The fulfillment of the Primal Vow is given to us as the nembutsu, "namu-amida-butsu." This is the Name-that-calls, penetrating to the core of my being—proud, stubborn, arrogant, deceitful, foolish. My hard ego-shell remains closed and refuses to open up, yet it cannot shut out the piercing call of nembutsu. The call resounds throughout the countless universes to ultimately awaken each of us to true and real life that flows silently within.

The nembutsu calls us without judging or condemning our refusal to hear; rather, it pursues us relentlessly with deep sorrow for the foolish self that chooses darkness. Yet, the ego-self ultimately undergoes a miraculous transformation, such that the very stubbornness cannot but become supple, open, and malleable. All this occurs as a natural process. That is, without "the practicer's intention all evils of past, present, and future are completely transformed into good. To transform means that evil is made into good without nullifying and eradicating evil."

Religious life does not require us to be "good" or "virtuous" as a condition. The only requirement is the openness to the beneficent, transforming power of the Primal Vow. And this occurs spontaneously when we awaken to true compassion that enables us to see our karmic reality—the limited, imperfect, foolish self. Such a self cannot ever hope to effect any change for the better by its own powers. "All this the Buddha already knew" and devised the means by which we become transformed into beings of highest good.

Once the process of change begins to takes place, we are shown ever more clearly the working of boundless compassion in relation to the ego-self rooted in countless samsaric lives. The sorrow of a karmic being, unable to effect any change by its own self-power, is bottomless. But even deeper is the sorrow of true compassion that identifies with such a hopeless one. The working of the Primal Vow lifts up the karmic burdens from our shoulders and carries us into the realm of lightness, clarity, and joy. Thus, in the darkest of hours, the most hopeless of situations, the most tragic of events, a new being is born to celebrate life.

> Such sorrow—
> The cry of true compassion
> Sinks into my hard ego.

AS IS: *SONO-MAMA*

25

The goal of Shin Buddhism is transcendence, contained in the deep aspiration to be born in the Pure Land. But it is ultimately redirected to this life, affirming that the here and now brims with infinite significance. In colloquial Japanese, such a reaffirmation of everyday life is called living *sono-mama* or *kono-mama*. Either phrase means simply life "as is" or "just right as is." A popular Shin poem expresses this realized state in simple, clear language:

> You, as you are, you're just right.
> Your face, body, name, surname,
> For you, they are just right.
>
> Whether poor or rich,
> Your parents, your children,
>   your daughter-in-law, your
>   grandchildren,
> They are, all for you, just right.

Happiness, unhappiness, joy and even sorrow.
For you, they are just right.

The life that you have tread is neither good nor bad,
For you, it is just right.

Whether you go to hell or to the Pure Land,
Wherever you go is just right.

Nothing to boast about, nothing to feel bad about,
Nothing above, nothing below.

Even the day and month that you die,
Even they are just right.

Life in which you walk together with Amida,
There's no way that it can't be just right.

When you receive your life as just right,
Then a deep and profound trust begins to open up.

Sono-mama is the everyday Japanese equivalent of suchness, thusness, or thingness, terms derived from Sanskrit originals (*tathata, tattva, dharmata,* respectively). It also incorporates the Chinese *tzu-jan,* translated by Arthur Waley as "self-so" or "always so." Whether it be sono-mama, suchness, or self-so, it cannot be fully understood within conventional dichotomous thinking. The reason is that such a way of thinking simply creates further divisions and contradictions, resulting in the fragmentation of life. This is what we call samsara, the very opposite of life as sono-mama.

Sono-mama is reality affirmed as it is without being distorted by calculative thinking. Since it is beyond the conventional subject-object duality, it is described as being nondual. Although sono-mama is beyond conceptual grasp, it can be manifested in a person's life. Anna Pavlova suggests something akin to this in the case of dancing; once she is said to have proclaimed, "The secret of becoming a fine dancer is to learn the theory and the technique thoroughly—then forget about it and just dance." Just dance sono-mama, but only after mastering the theory and technique.

The person who chooses the Shin path devotes hours, days, and years to the interior practice of deep hearing. This results in the intimacy with the Primal Vow, especially the reason for Dharmakara Bodhisattva's identification with our karmic life. This initial stage of deep hearing is like mastering the theory. But this must be followed by the saying of nembutsu, the practice equivalent to mastering technique in dance. Deep hearing and recitative nembutsu. After that everything must be forgotten and the person must "just live," but now live with awareness, sensitivity, and grace. While the mastery of dance is but one aspect of a person's life, the mastery of nembutsu path involves the whole person. The interior practice of deep hearing, learning and forgetting, ultimately leads to a life of sono-mama.

But we must not forget the words of the myokonin Ichitaro, who lived such a life: "Everything is as-it-is (sono-mama) means this: We undergo all kinds of difficult and painful practices. We travel to all kinds of places and then discover that we didn't have to do a thing. That things are as-they-are. It's not that everything is as-it-is, without us having tried anything. Everything is as-it-is after we've broken our bones, trying everything." This is the challenge that Shinran makes when he writes:

More difficult than believing in all the teachings
Is entrusting the self to the Universal Vow:
"The most difficult among all difficulties,
Nothing more difficult than this," so it is said.

In sum, sono-mama is true entrusting being manifested in everyday life. It cannot be programmed by willpower or decided by
rational deliberation. It comes naturally and spontaneously as we
open ourselves up to the working of great compassion, letting it
shape and inform our lives the way it is meant to be.

DUALITY

26

Conventional thinking is characterized by all kinds of duality: self and other, right and wrong, good and bad, like and dislike, beautiful and ugly, birth and death, and so on. These conceptual distinctions are necessary and useful, but they are all relative viewpoints made from a limited perspective. As long as we don't mistake these words for a concrete, unmovable reality, there is no problem. But we seem to always confuse the two, infusing words with powerful emotions and grasping them as substantial. We thus create our world of delusion, full of words and concepts, existing completely separate from reality. We then come to accept conflict, competition, jealousy, greed, acquisitiveness, and aggression as the norm of life.

The problem of dualistic, or dichotomous, thinking is posed in the opening verse of the Zen text "Believing in the Mind":

The Perfect Way knows no difficulties,
Except that it refuses to make preferences;
Only when freed from hate and love,
It reveals itself fully and without disguise.

Contained within dualistic thinking are several problems that may not be obvious at first glance. First is the hidden self-centeredness. The ego-self is the center of the world, and judgments about the world are made from this standpoint. This naturally limits our ability to see things, including the self, as they are. And when we try to make the world move according to our egocentric needs, conflicts with others are inevitable.

Second is the lack of self-knowledge. The knowing subject can never see itself, because knowledge in the dichotomous framework means objectifying things, including the self. This means that the more we try to know ourselves, the more we objectify the self. And the knowing subject recedes forever beyond our grasp.

Third is mistaking words for reality. When we are unaware that words and concepts are arbitrary constructs, interwoven into dualistic thinking, we cling to them as if they are real. When our emotional life becomes caught up with these words and concepts, we plunge deeper into samsara.

I still recall one of the first big fights that I had with my wife and partner, Alice. It happened some years ago one early summer evening, when we lived in Los Angeles. We received a telephone call and had to go out on an emergency. Alice dressed our son, Mark, who was two years old at that time. An active little boy, he perspired easily, but she made him wear a jacket that evening. Thinking that it would be too warm for him, I took it off and put on a sweater. Alice saw this, took off the sweater, and put the jacket back on Mark. I yelled at her, saying that he would run around, surely perspire, and catch a cold. I took off the jacket and made him wear the sweater. Then she really got upset, jerked the sweater off, and shouted at me with a barrage of accusations: You don't know what's best for your son, you're never home, you rarely play with him, you're an ungrateful husband, unloving father, and on and on. I, too, exploded with angry expletives that I can't even remember today, but I do remember yelling at the end, "I should've married your sister!" In the meanwhile our son was running around in the front yard wearing just a T-shirt, perspiring and catching a cold.

Here we see two people with good intentions, concerned with a potential problem and proposing to do what is best. But we both act as if we know what's best for the situation, unaware of the hidden land mines. First, each views the situation from a particular perspective that is self-centered and one-sided. When a disagreement arises, it's always the other's fault. This simply deepens the conflict, and a resolution becomes even more difficult.

Second, as the conflict grows, one clings ever more stubbornly to one's viewpoint. There is complete lack of self-reflection concerning one's own shortcomings. This inability to be self-critical is part of the darkness of ignorance that we carry into all of our dealings. Due to this darkness, we easily erupt with self-righteous anger and create emotional havoc for everyone, especially oneself. We then sink deeper into the morass of total confusion.

Third, in such a confrontation words are thrown out thoughtlessly, often just to vent our frustration or simply to hurt the other. The careless misuse of words ignites even greater violent reactions. Words are infused with powerful emotions, take on a life of their own and beyond rational control. They can even reach a completely twisted and hurtful culmination, as in my fight with Alice. When we mistake words for reality, we are subject to the tyranny of words.

As long as we seek solutions dualistically, always blaming the other and never reflecting on oneself, there is no end to disagreements, conflicts, and violence. If we had paused for a moment that early summer evening in Los Angeles, an unhappy incident could have been avoided. Alice and I have different karmic histories that have shaped our lives, temperaments, sensitivities, and even body temperatures. When we retire for the night, for example, she likes to sleep with a gown under several blankets with windows closed, whereas I prefer only my underwear, a single sheet, and windows wide open. This obvious difference, even if only physiological, already shows that Alice and I will have two different perspectives on many things. Disagreements are only natural because of different karmic histories, but that is not the problem. The problem is the entrenchment in one's position, refusal to acknowledge the other's viewpoint, and becoming adamant about one's correctness.

Since dualistic thinking is our common lot as beings in samsara, we cannot become free of its binding powers through our limited intellect. Speaking of the way he handled his degenerative joint disease, Brian Schultz, who was quoted earlier, states, "People think that once the symptoms are gone, you're all well. But the healing goes on and just gets more intense." The same holds true for the awakening to one's karmic limitations. As we grow in awareness through deep hearing, the fathomless nature of our ignorance becomes more and more evident. By virtue of the light of great compassion we are able to see more deeply into the human condition, so that we might become more real, true, and compassionate.

The words of Shinran come back to us repeatedly, each time

we make mistakes in life: "All this the Buddha already knew and called us foolish beings filled with blind passion." When we acknowledge our karmic reality, illuminated by great compassion, our transformation takes place and the possibility of change occurs for the first time. Shinran's words are followed by the reassuring words: "When we realize that the compassionate vow of Other Power is for beings like ourselves, the Vow becomes even more reliable and dependable."

In Western thought we also have thinkers who have questioned the validity of dualistic thinking. One of the leading critics is Friedrich Nietzsche, who advocated a wholesale rethinking of our philosophical assumptions in order to overcome the nihilism that he saw coming with the advent of modernity. He questions the reliance on conceptual thought, characteristic of dualistic thinking. In *The Will to Power,* a collection of Nietzsche's mature thoughts, he states:

> If we give up the concept "subject" and "object," then also the concept "substance"—and as a consequence also the various modifications of it, e.g., "matter," "spirit," and other hypothetical entities, "eternity and immutability of matter," etc. We have got rid of materiality. (No. 552d)

Nietzsche rejects our tendency to reify concepts ("materiality"), whether subject, object, substance, matter, spirit, eternity, or immutability that are the building blocks of a dualistic worldview. The root cause of this phenomenon is connected to our unquestioned belief in a substantial, enduring self. Such a self is negated by Nietzsche as nothing more than a product of grammatical habit:

That when there is thought there has to be something
that "thinks" is simply a formulation of our grammatical custom that adds a doer to every deed. (No. 484)

To assume without question that the self exists as a metaphysical
entity goes against reality.

The contemporary Jewish philosopher Martin Buber speaks
of two kinds of relations, I-It and I-Thou, that constitute our
world. From the Buddhist perspective we might say that the I-It
relationship is based on duality in which the other is treated as a
mere object. In contrast, the I-Thou relationship is nondual,
such that the divine is seen in all things without any discrimination. The goal of the Buddhist life is to affirm all existence as
possessing Buddha-nature. To speak of suchness or thatness is to
be in an I-Thou relationship with all people and all things,
animate and inanimate.

It seems that Tillich was also aware of the problem of duality and nonduality. He is critical of the dualistic approach to
God when he states, "If you start with the question whether
God does or does not exist, you can never reach Him." Faith also
cannot be realized within the subject-object framework: "The
more idolatrous a faith the less it is able to overcome the cleavage
between subject and object." Tillich's version of nonduality appears in the following statement: "God can never be an object
without being at the same time subject."

In Mahayana Buddhism the technical term for dualistic
thinking is *vijnana*, which must undergo a radical conversion into
its opposite, *prajna*, the wisdom of nonduality. The Zen text
cited at the beginning sums up this wisdom as follows:

> In the higher realm of true Suchness
> There is neither "self" nor "other";

When direct identification is sought,
We can only say, "Not Two."

What does "Not Two" or nonduality really mean? What does it
have to do with self-knowledge? What is its relation to knowing
reality as-it-is in the world of duality? What are its practical
consequences?

NONDUALITY

27

Nonduality is not the opposite of duality, nor is it a simplistic negation of duality. Nonduality affirms duality from a higher standpoint. It is not an abstract concept but lived reality. But the difficulty is in understanding it, because we have here a double exposure, so to speak, of duality and nonduality. The complexity of the realized state when approached from conventional thinking causes problems for us. What I refer to as double exposure may be illustrated by taking examples that are readily accessible.

William James in his *Varieties of Religious Experience* discusses a number of nondual experiences. He describes a musician who becomes totally engrossed in his playing: "He may suddenly reach a point at which pleasure in the technique of the art entirely falls away and in some moment of inspiration he becomes the instrument through which music flows." Here there is no separation between the musician and his instrument (nonduality), although both are distinct and separate entities (duality).

The Chinese poet, Su Tung-p'o of the eleventh century, articulates nonduality in his poem:

> When Yu-k'o painted bamboo
> He saw bamboo only, never people.
> Did I say he saw no people
> So rapt he forgot even himself—
> He himself became bamboo,
> Putting out fresh growth endlessly.
> Chuang Tzu no longer with us,
> Who can fathom this uncanny power?

In the same vein, Basho writes on the art of haiku: "Go to the pine if you want to learn about the pine, or to the bamboo if you want to learn about the bamboo. And in doing so, you must leave your subjective preoccupation with yourself. . . . However well phrased your poetry may be, if your feeling is not natural—if the object and yourself are separate—then your poetry is not true poetry but your subjective counterfeit." Both Yu-k'o and Basho are independent from the bamboo (duality), yet they both "become" bamboo (nonduality). Their self-centered subjectivity is given up in order to tap the fountain of creativity.

Nonduality is also achieved by gifted athletes, as evidenced by countless examples from *In the Zone: Transcendent Experience in Sports* by Michele Murphy and Rhea White. The superstar Magic Johnson, for example, once said after a rigorous practice session: "Basketball was like a part of me, like another arm. By then, I just had the touch, and it was as if the ball wasn't there." Here there is no separation of player and basketball. Magic

Johnson dribbles the ball (duality), but it is an extension of his body (nonduality).

These examples make the notion of nonduality simple to understand, but their inadequacy is indicated by the subtitle of the book, *Transcendent Experience in Sports*. That is, although a person may be so attuned to the world that no dichotomy exists between self and world, actor and act, it is confined to a particular realm of human activity, the world of athletics. An insightful comment made by the former star quarterback John Brodie spells out the fundamental problem:

> (Athletes) don't have a workable philosophy or understanding to support the kind of thing they get into while they are playing. They don't have the words for it. So after a game you see some of them coming down, making fools of themselves sometimes, coming way down in their tone level. But during the game they come way up. A missing ingredient for many people, I guess, is that they don't have a supporting philosophy or discipline for a better life.

In Buddhism nonduality is an entirely different type of experience from the examples given above. The contrast may be summed up as follows. First, religious practice involves intensive training of the whole person, not just of one aspect, with the explicit purpose of realizing nonduality in mind and body, in thinking, feeling, and willing. Second, as a consequence, it can be manifested at will and at any time, applicable to diverse areas of activity rather than simply to one aspect, whether sports, dance, or artistic achievement. Third, nonduality is most important in interpersonal relationships in which the needs of the other take

priority over one's own needs. And the fulfillment experienced
by the other is one's own fulfillment.

The wisdom of nonduality is based on a de-centered form
of knowing, called *prajna,* such that the other is seen from within
its own center and not from the standpoint of the ego-self. This
is itself *karuna* or compassion, whereby the other is affirmed
before oneself. This forms the crux of the story of Dharmakara
Bodhisattva, who identifies with suffering beings and dedicates
endless practice, contemplation, and vows to cure their karmi-
cally created disease.

Historically speaking, nonduality in Buddhism is used primarily in three ways. The first is practical, contained in the
Middle Way taught in the Buddha's first sermon at Benares. The
Middle Way of nonduality negates the two extremes of hedo-
nism and asceticism and advocates a commonsense approach to
life. This develops later into a sophisticated critique of such
concepts as eternalism and annihilationism, being and nonbeing,
and samsara and nirvana. But the Middle Way is basically a
practical method of coping with the world, using analytical tools
to deal with contradictions.

The second is philosophical. Here nonduality is synonymous with such central Buddhist concepts as emptiness, suchness, reality-limit, dependent co-origination, the inexpressible,
nirvana, and so on. While all of these terms are sometimes
interpreted abstractly, they, in fact, result from the pragmatic
application of the Middle Way principle. Implicit in this usage
of nonduality is the affirmation of the world of duality where
mutual responsibility is the binding thread. Everyday distinctions are fully recognized, free of all egocentric perceptions that
distort reality. The world is seen in its pristine form; the suchness of people, things, events, nature, and all phenomena are
affirmed in endless interconnectedness.

The third is the religious use of this term found in Pure Land Buddhism. Nonduality sums up the relationship between sentient beings and Amida Buddha. Sentient beings and Amida Buddha are two, yet they are one. They are one, yet two. In their oneness, the two are clearly distinct and separate. This should be differentiated from an uncritical oneness that negates distinctions. This nondual relationship is expressed by Saichi, when he muses:

> Wind and air are two,
> But it is one wind, one air.
> Amida and I are two,
> But the compassion of Namu-amida-butsu is one.

In traditional Shin doctrine this nondual relationship is expressed as the oneness of *ki* (potential) and *ho* (dharmic reality). Ki is each of us as *namu,* and ho is *amida-butsu.* Here again nonduality affirms duality, such that while sentient beings and Amida are separate and distinct, they become one in great compassion.

INTERDEPENDENCE

28

Freed of the constricting worldview based on dualistic thinking, nonduality uncovers the boundless universe of interconnectedness and interdependence. This is more elemental than anything
that human beings can intellectually conceive or
imagine. The Dalai Lama makes the point very
simply and clearly, seeing this fact in the smallest
of creatures:

> Interdependence is a fundamental law of
> nature. Many of the smallest insects are
> social beings who, without any religion,
> law or education, survive by mutual co-
> operation based on an innate recognition
> of their interconnectedness.

When the world is seen from the conventional
dualistic standpoint, there is only one center: me,
the ego-self. To assume that everything should

revolve around this self is to distort the reality of things, including the self, as they are. As a consequence, all kinds of false discriminations, projected from this static center, abound. But when the world is affirmed from a nondualistic, de-centered, and awakened viewpoint, each reality is seen not only as is—an integral part of interconnected and interdependent life—but is responsible for transforming the world to accord with that vision.

A simple story, coming from the Shin tradition, exemplifies the life lived within this reality of interdependence. The myokonin Genza had a maid who returned home for a brief visit. Genza sent a sack of sweet potato with her to be given to her parents. When she came back from her visit, she said to Genza, "My parents thank you for the sweet potatoes." Whereupon he replied, "Don't thank me, thank the sweet potatoes."

Genza acknowledges the interdependence of all things; he does not see himself as the sole center of life. The maid, her parents, the sweet potatoes, and Genza himself—each is equally a center to be affirmed. Genza was generous with the gift, but the sweet potatoes made his act of generosity possible, and the parents who acknowledged the gift completed Genza's act. So, why should only Genza get credit? In this brief exchange we see the practice of selfless giving illustrated within the context of interdependence. That is, the act of giving has been accomplished free of any one-sided attachments. Such a giving accords with what the Buddhists call the purity of three factors—no giver, no gift, and no receiver—in the act of true generosity.

Such an understanding has been part of everyday custom among traditional Buddhist families. I remember growing up as a child, whenever we received a gift for any occasion, we had to first place it before the family altar and with our palms together bow to the Buddha. Only then could we open the gift. Thanking the Buddha is acknowledging the vast web of life that makes giving and receiving possible. The focus is shifted away from attachments to the giver, the gift, or the receiver and directed to all the forces that made it possible.

Interdependence is not an abstract concept but must be embodied and lived in everyday life. In fact, in the awareness of and the freedom from egocentric perceptions, one sees things, including the self, as they are with clarity and precision. This world is full of distinctions, yet each reality is affirmed as part of the vast network of interdependence that sustains all of us.

This fact of interconnectedness has permeated the lives of East Asian peoples in various degrees, but it awaits to be articulated in contemporary terms. Its application, however, will require imagination and boldness, for the problems facing the world are complex and intertwined with many factors: overpopulation, pollution, deforestation and desertification, shrinking food sources, declining fossil fuel, destruction of the ozone layer, international trade conflicts, and multi-ethnic wars. But we must begin somewhere.

The Zen master Thich Nhat Hanh suggests a very practical way to cultivate the awareness of interdependence, or interbeing, as he calls it. Derived from the *Avatamsaka Sutra*, he expands upon it in his *The Blooming of a Lotus*. One of his well-known sayings is to be repeated:

> Aware of myself picking up
> An autumn leaf,
> I breathe in.

> Touching the wonderful
> Interdependent nature of that leaf,
> I breathe out.

Aware of myself alive
Here and now,
I breathe in.

Touching the wonderful
Interdependent nature of life in me,
And around me, I breathe out.

Interdependence with nature is acknowledged throughout the world, but in earlier times it was a personal, intimate experience. When woodcutters felled trees, for example, it was said that they could hear the mournful sound of the trees as they fell to the ground. Alice Walker in her *Temple of My Familiar* mentions such a sense of communion in South America. Talking about a priest named Jesus, she writes: "Jesus was such a priest I used to feel as if the trees fell before him to be blessed, because, clearly cutting them down was for him a torture comparable to being cut down himself. They were sobbing all the while, Jesus and his trees. He had known them all his whole life. And for all his lifetime before."

An awareness of interconnectedness is deeply embedded in the Japanese psyche, as expressed in a popular saying: "Even the brushing of sleeves between passersby reveals deep connections in past lives." When people traveled on foot in premodern times, they would encounter strangers on the road or in wayside inns. They believed that the meetings were not mere happenstance, for no matter how brief and passing an encounter, it was due to some profound karmic links from countless past lives. Because of such unknown ties that reason could never fathom, people would be sensitive to each other's thoughts, feelings, and needs. Chance meetings and unexpected coincidences have far-

reaching significance beyond any rational comprehension, something that Carl Jung tried to suggest in his idea of synchronicity.

Interdependence is at the core of all religious life, articulated
as the felt sense of the unity with all existence. Ichitaro, the
myokonin, describes it as follows:

> True entrusting means that you're able to truly relate to
> another being. Not only human beings but with plants
> and animals. Even those things that cannot speak, you're
> able to hear their feelings. Namu-amida-butsu.

The vast network of interdependence is not only spatial but also
temporal. It connects people in the present with those who have
gone before and those who will come after. In such an understanding of interconnectedness one's appreciation for life is limitless. The poet Mitsuo Aida writes:

> My father and mother, altogether two.
> Parents of my father and mother, altogether four.
> Parents of parents, altogether eight.
> If I count in this way,
> Back to ten generations, altogether 1,024.
> What about back to twenty generations?
> To my surprise, over one million people.
> From infinite past, a life rally baton has passed on.
> Here, now I live with my baton.
> This is your life!
> This is my life!

This worldview is at the basis of Shinran's identification with all
of life: "I, Shinran, have never even once uttered the nembutsu

for the sake of my father and mother. The reason is that all beings have been fathers and mothers, brothers and sisters, in the timeless process of birth-and-death." (*Tannisho* V) Here Shinran negates filial piety to his parents, central to the value system of medieval Japan. Instead, he identifies with all beings in time and space. This does not exclude his parents, for they are at the very center of the network of interdependence.

Interdependence, or dependent co-origination, received its most sophisticated formulation in Hua-yen Buddhism. Among its well-known doctrine is the master-attendant interrelationship. The two are mutually and simultaneously dependent and responsible for each other. That is, when one is affirmed as master, the other becomes its attendant. But, at the same time the roles are reversed; the other is affirmed as master and one becomes an attendant to serve the other. The interrelationship is forever changing, fluid, and subtle, beyond any rigid hierarchies and negating any self-importance.

Interdependence is an elemental truth. When one awakens to this fact, compassion that sustains us strikes us with full force, and we are made to respond to the world with the same compassion. Crucial to living this life of interdependence is a new sense of selfhood, radically different from conventional views.

SELF AS DYNAMIC FLOW

29

南
無
阿
彌
陀
佛

The vast network of interconnectedness comes
alive with a self-understanding that is entirely inconsistent with modern assumptions about the
self. This was made clear to me in a conversation
I had several years ago with a high-ranking
Aikido instructor from Japan at a summer camp
in Massachusetts. He made an interesting observation, saying, "In America you talk about martial arts as self-defense, but the aim of martial
arts is to train yourself to the point that there is
no self to defend. The term self-defense is very
strange to me." Strange, indeed, because the purpose of Aikido, a product of the East Asian
worldview, is to reduce reliance on ego-strength
and train one's *ki*-power, such that every movement becomes circular or spherical attuned to
the universal life force. Unlike the popular concept of a confrontational self-defense, Aikido

techniques form a dynamic sphere that deflects any direct blows, forcing the attacker, already off balance, to fall by his own momentum.

In East Asian cultures the dynamic flow of ki (*ch'i* in Chinese) forms the vital center of a person. It is neither mental nor physical, yet infuses both mind and body. While forming the core of a person, it is entirely different from the ego-self. Thus, for example, in vernacular Japanese ki is frequently used as the subject of a sentence. Instead of saying, "I don't want to go," a person says "ki refuses to move." Instead of "he is undependable," "his ki constantly changes." Instead of "I am upset," "ki is upset." Instead of "I understand," "ki understands." Instead of "he is a coward," "his ki is weak." Instead of "she is brave," "her ki is powerful." In brief, there are countless such phrases in which the subject is the unifying ki-energy, never a self-conscious agent.

In contrast to such an understanding, the indisputable agent of action in the English language is the self. For example, the *Random House Dictionary of the English Language* (Second Edition Unabridged, 1983) lists approximately eleven hundred compounds for self. It begins with "self-abandonment" and ends with "self-wrought." This focus on the "self" may explain the reason why Western interest in Buddhism so far has been mainly psychotherapeutic. The primary goal is seen as health, wealth, and well-being. Buddhism does contain a strong dose of the psychological, but its primary concern is confronting the problems of suffering, evil, and death that may have no rational answers.

Something similar to the dynamic flow of ki-energy may be found in the thought of William James. He describes the conventional understanding of self in terms of material self, social self, and spiritual self. First is the self identified in relation to

material possessions—body, clothes, family, and so on; second is
self in social relationships—fame, honor, and so forth; and third
includes soul, spirit, and psyche. But these are all objectified,
conceptual notions. The living self is the stream of consciousness or stream of thought that flows below them. A similar
understanding of a dynamic self occurs simultaneously in the
philosophies of Henri Bergson (élan vital) in France and Kitaro
Nishida (pure experience) in Japan. The three thinkers represent
a break in traditional philosophy focusing on metaphysics, although each goes on his separate way.

What all this suggests is that the proper understanding of
interdependence requires a radically different orientation to
"self." When the basic self is a stream of consciousness that can
never be objectified, or the flow of ki that is neither mental nor
physical, we naturally become free of reifying "self." We, then,
become liberated not only from "self" but from the tyranny of
words that cause the fragmentation of our world.

When the integrity of the new sense of selfhood is thus
established, free from any conceptualized notions and false discriminations, one has embodied the Buddha Dharma in one's
being. The somatic embodiment appears in the recourse to the
five senses to describe the religious life. Thus, we find, for example, frequent references to the *taste* of Buddha Dharma, the *flavor*
of true entrusting, the *fragrance* of myokonin, the *touch* of compassionate light, *seeing* the heart of compassion, *hearing* the light of
compassion, and so on. Religiosity at its depth affects our body
and impacts the five senses.

O Saichi, tell us what kind of taste
Is the taste of Namu-amida-butsu.
The taste of Namu-amida-butsu is—

A joy filling up the bosom,
A joy filling up the liver,
Like the rolling swell of the sea,
No words—just the utterance, "oh, oh!"

ALL IS A CIRCLE

30

The universal symbol of wholeness is the circle and its variants: sphere, disc, ring, orbit, wheel, globe, mandala. This is true of the world when we look around us. Flowers, plants, and trees are full of curves all seeking the rays of the sun. Graceful human movements are circular or spherical in dance, ritual motion, athletics, martial arts, tea ceremony, floral arrangement. Games of all sorts use some form of round object—basketball, tennis ball, golf ball, bowling ball. System thinkers assert that "reality is made up of circles but we see straight lines." The universe consists of whirlpool galaxies, planetary orbits, and the diurnal cycle.

When our son was two and a half years old, he drew an almost perfect circle on a small blackboard put up for him. It was amazing for one so young to do this, so I took a snapshot of his drawing. Some years later when I showed it to a

Jungian analyst, he remarked that anyone so young who can draw a near perfect circle is well grounded in wholeness; and no matter what happens later in life, even if he goes astray at times, he will always return to the center. Not bad information for a parent to hear.

When I was in my thirties, I took up Aikido because I was fascinated with its nonviolent philosophy. I soon learned that all Aikido movements are spherical. It does not teach any offensive techniques, such as kicks, blows, strikes, or thrusts. The purpose of training is to become like a round ball, curbing our angular, linear, erratic movements. The same holds true for T'ai Chi Chuan, which is a more deliberate version of Aikido. They share a common philosophy based on centering, ambidextrous movements, and flowing together with the ki of the universe.

Violence is inevitable in the dualistic encounter between the attacker and attacked. In contrast, Aikido is based on nonduality; that is, the attacker is absorbed into the swift spherical movements of the one attacked. The attacker and attacked become one. This is the reason that one never hears of Aikido contests or tournaments to determine who is the best.

In his absorbing little book, *Everyday Suchness,* Gyomay Kubose, founder of the Chicago Buddhist Temple, reflects on a small, smooth stone he found while being confined in the internment camp in Wyoming during the Second World War. He writes:

In this round stone, I feel a peaceful, harmonious and perfect character—a character acquired through many years of hardships. As I feel its smoothness and roundness, I know that it was not so in the beginning. It must have had many sharper corners when it was cracked off from the mother stone and began its long journey down the rivers and creeks enduring the heat, the rainstorms and the freezing Wyoming winters. For how long, it is hard to tell, perhaps for thousands of years; and as it was rolled and tossed with the other rocks and stones, it was polished and the sharp corners disappeared.

Kubose reflects on the stone and speaks with a voice of a person truly attuned to nature: "As I see many sharp corners and roughness in me, I feel that I am much smaller and inferior to the stone. This little stone on my desk is, indeed, a great teacher to me."

According to informed sources, among the 550 Native American languages there is not a single word for "religion," but we find constant references to the circle and to holy power. The circle is part of everyday life—tepee, sacred pipe, purification lodge, sun dance, ceremonial disc, and sacred wheel patterns. And holy power, *wakan tanka,* is found in man, tree, buffalo, rock, sacred pipe, and so on.

One of the most popular religious texts among college students today is *Black Elk Speaks* as recorded by John Neihardt. Black Elk shouldered the destiny of his people in the face of the Wasichus' destruction of his culture. He ultimately failed to protect them, but the impact of his spirituality still affects many people today. Among his recollections is the reference to his Oglala Sioux nation as the sacred hoop:

> You have noticed that everything an Indian does is in a circle, and that is because the Power of the World always works in circles. . . . The sky is round, and I have heard that the earth is round like a ball, and so are all the stars. The wind, in its greatest power, whirls. Birds make their nests in circles, for theirs is the same religion

as ours. The sun comes forth and goes down again in a
circle. The moon does the same, and both are round.
. . . Our tepees were round like the nests of birds, and
these were always set in a circle, the nation's hoop, a nest
of many nests, where the Great Spirit meant for us to
hatch our children. But the Wasichus have put us in
those square boxes.

Black Elk here contrasts the circle, expressing the vitality of his
people, and the square boxes suffocating their life.

Besides the imagery of the circle, Black Elk's story contains
numerous references to the number four. He speaks of four
directions, four seasons, four parts of a plant, four periods of
life, four chiefs, four horses, four ascents, four above worlds, four
kinds of gods, and so on. The intimate relationship between the
number four and the circle was noted by Carl Jung when he saw
this pattern recurring in the drawings of his patients in the
process of individuation. They invariably drew variations of a
circle with four parts, a pattern basic to the mandala. Jung went
on to discover the mandalas as a common symbol in world
cultures—Native American, alchemy, medieval Christianity,
Taoism, Hinduism, and Buddhism.

The mandala in Tibetan Buddhism and Japanese Shingon
incorporates the phenomenal world of samsara with its polarities
and identifies it with the undifferentiated core of nirvana. The
contemplation of the mandala provides a channel by which the
meditator realizes union with the cosmic Buddha. The process
of realization may differ among the various traditions, but its
ultimate goal is to realize the oneness of the microcosm and
macrocosm.

A concrete form of this practice is found in the moon-disc

contemplation of Shingon Buddhism. Consciousness is visual-
ized as the full moon, brilliant and unsullied, which is gradually
expanded to cover the horizon of life. One then overcomes the
duality of subject and object, manifesting the bright fullness of
the moon in one's own being and consciousness. The aim is to
cultivate compassion for all of existence, including oneness with
nature. Saigyo, the medieval monk-poet, practiced the moon-
disc contemplation and wrote many poems referring to the
moon. One of his poems reads:

> Over the mountain edges
> Slips the moon;
> Watching it
> I too enter
> The west of my heart.

Saigyo has internalized the contemplation of the moon, signifying the consummation of life. He calls it entering the "west,"
referring to the Pure Land, located in the westerly direction that
signifies transcendence of samsara.

In the Zen tradition one of the favorite symbols for calligraphy scrolls is a circle, known as *enso*, drawn with a swift brush
stroke. It is said to represent the "original face," and it is used
graphically to depict emptiness, a term derived from the Sanskrit
word for "zero" (*sunya*), one of the great discoveries made by
ancient Indian mathematicians. But it also has profound implications for religious and philosophic thought in Buddhism. A
contemporary appropriation of emptiness is found in *Religion and
Nothingness* by Keiji Nishitani. Drawing on both Western and
Eastern sources, he elaborates on the imagery of a boundless
circle:

Since there is no circumference on the field of sunyata, "All are One" cannot be symbolized by a circle (or a sphere). . . . It is, as it were, a circumferenceless center, a center that is only center and nothing else, a center on a field of emptiness. That is to say, on the field of sunyata *the center is everywhere.*

Such an imagery seems to have been universal, since we find examples of the boundless circle in other traditions. A favorite metaphor among medieval Christian mystics, for example, was "the circle without a circumference whose center is everywhere." Although ascribed to various medieval mystics, it appears as early as the twelfth century in the writings of Alan of Lille. In his words, "God is the intelligible sphere whose centre is everywhere and whose circumference is nowhere." Black Elk also is purported to have said, "Anywhere is the center of the world," even while standing on the highest mountain in the Black Hills and seeing round about beneath him the whole hoop of the world.

In Pure Land Buddhism the compassion of Amida is described as a great wheel or orb of light that is boundless, illuminating our existence here and now but centered on foolish karmic beings. Shinran writes:

Amida has passed through ten kalpas
Since realizing Buddhahood,
The wheel of dharmakaya is boundless
Shining on the blind and ignorant of the world.

The liberating wheel of light is boundless;
Each person it touches, so it is taught,
Is freed from attachments to being and non-being,

So take refuge in Amida, the enlightenment that sees all
equally.

Shinran refers to the center of a circle without a circumference as
isshiji (one-child-earth). This indicates that each person is the
primary concern of great compassion, just as an only child is the
sole focus of parental love. Genshin, one of the great teachers of
Japanese Pure Land, states:

> The Buddha's regard for each sentient being with eyes of
> compassion is equal, as though each one were his only
> child; hence I take refuge in and worship the unsur-
> passed mother of great compassion.

This is expressed in a deeply personal confession by Shinran:
"When I ponder on the compassionate vow of Amida, established through five kalpas of profound thought, it was for myself, Shinran, alone."

KNOW THYSELF

31

南無阿彌陀佛

The Delphic pronouncement "Know Thyself" is applicable to many religious and philosophical teachings. Stories abound in Buddhist literature preaching the centrality of self-understanding. But to truly know oneself is a perilous matter, fraught with all kinds of temptations and obstacles. Foremost among them is our uncanny ability to delude ourselves, that through some extraordinary experience—ecstatic visions, paranormal powers, mystical clairvoyance—we achieve a kind of self-knowledge. In fact, Buddhism says that they only deepen our self-delusion.

Many years ago in a school textbook I saw a cartoon of carpetbaggers, those calculating Northerners who went to the South to reap profits during the post-Civil War period of reconstruction. They carried their belongings in satchels, one in front of them and one in back, tied with straps slung over their shoulders. They could see the satchel in front, but never the satchel in the back. Self-knowledge is analogous to this. We, for example, readily admit to faults that we know about, but never to those we ourselves can't see, no matter how obvious they may be to other people.

This problem is rooted in the conventional, dualistic thinking that divides reality into subject and object, knower and known. It is impossible to truly know oneself as long as the knower has to objectify itself. In such knowing, the knower consistently recedes into the background and is nowhere to be found. This dilemma has been pointed out by many philosophers throughout the world. We find it in expressions such as the eye cannot see itself, the knife cannot cut itself, and the lip cannot kiss itself.

The only way that we can know ourselves is to *become* ourselves. Knowing through becoming means complete mastery, because there is no conceptual gap between the knower and known, or between the "dancer and the dance," to quote William Butler Yeats. In Asian traditions this is sometimes referred to as knowing with the body; it is also referred to as embodied knowledge or experiential wisdom. Since knowing through becoming involves the body, it exceeds rational comprehension.

I once heard a lecture by a distinguished Japanese psychiatrist who applied this principle of knowing as becoming in his clinical practice. He said that, for example, when he had a client with a Shin background, he would require the person to read a selected passage from the *Tannisho* one hundred times. Likewise, a patient coming from a Christian background would be asked to read chapters and verses from the New Testament one hundred times. If this did not ensure a deep, intimate reading, then he would require that the most significant phrases or passages be copied one hundred times. This inevitably made the reader identify himself or herself completely with what was read.

The following passage from *Tannisho* IV, for example, may resonate with a person who is trying to help a friend in distress: "In this life no matter how much pity and sympathy we may feel for others, it is impossible to help another as we truly wish; thus our compassion is inconsistent and limited." This is more than just reading a text, for one not only knows what is stated but experiences everything that is said. According to Hans-Georg Gadamer, the same holds true in reading Christian scriptures: "The understanding of a text has not begun at all as long as the text remains mute. . . . When it does begin to speak, however, it does not simply speak its word, always the same, in lifeless rigidity, but gives ever new answers to the person who questions it and poses ever new questions to him who answers it. To understand a text is to come to understand oneself in a kind of dialogue."

One of the primary functions of Buddhist scriptures, thus, is to bring to light the hidden aspects of the reader that is not readily recognized. The repeated reading of scripture, however, sooner or later opens up intimate truths about the reader that have been previously unknown. This sets the stage for knowing as becoming. When one begins to read scriptures in this way, one can also read everyday experiences as instructive and enlightening.

Masao Hanada, a close friend of this psychiatrist, told me the following episode. As a young man, he devoted himself to the practice of nembutsu, but he was not satisfied with it. Being very idealistic, he joined a religious community on the outskirts of Kyoto. This particular community was based upon the teachings of world religions and advocated service to society as its main practice. It was to be done quietly and without any publicity. To cultivate humility, they devoted themselves to cleaning public latrines in the city of Kyoto.

One early morning Hanada was on his knees, scrubbing and cleaning the floor of the toilet, when he looked up and saw well-dressed businessmen, hurrying to their offices with their brief-cases. In that instant he thought, "I'm better than all of them!" At the same time, a sense of deep shame overcame him. Here he was supposed to be practicing humility, yet manifesting arro-gance, asserting his superiority. He immediately recognized his true reality, his defiled I, which made him truly humble.

As limited human beings we cannot know everything about the world. This is especially true today with the flood of infor-mation on the Internet inundating our lives. But without authen-tic self-knowledge, our life would be incomplete. Without truly knowing oneself, how can we really be happy? How can we ever know the hearts and minds of other people? How can we ever appreciate the love extended to us by others? How can we really die when our time on this earth comes to an end?

HELL IS MY
ONLY HOME

32

The awareness of self as a limited karmic being dawns on us as we try to live the highest ethical life. And the more dedicated we are in pursuing religious life, the greater our awareness of dismal shortcomings. This may sound negative, but in fact it is our true reality coming to the fore. Such is the background of Shinran's famous confession: "Since I am absolutely incapable of any religious practice, hell is my only home." (*Tannisho* II) What does this mean? What is hell (*naraka*) in the Buddhist view? What happens when one ends up in hell?

In Buddhism hell does not exist as a place; it is created by each individual's thought, speech, and action. Hell is the consequence of karmic life for which each person alone is accountable. No one else should be blamed for one's past history, present circumstances, or future happenings. The law of karma is the ultimate form of personal responsibility, and its validity is to be tested through rigorous self-examination and applied to one's own existential predicament. The principle of karma should never be applied to others, as found in such thoughtless expressions as "That's his karma," when another person experiences misfortune.

According to the Buddhist worldview, unenlightened life is basically an aimless wandering through various states of being, called the six realms. The six in ascending order are the realms of hellish existence, hungry ghosts, beasts, fighting demons, human beings, and heavenly beings. They are found here and now when we experience moments of insufferable anguish and pain (realm of hell), when we are driven by unquenchable and uncontrollable desires (realm of hungry ghosts), when we fail to live by ethical and moral guidelines (realm of beasts), when we are driven by violent fits of anger (realm of fighting demons), when we abide by social norms (realm of human beings), when we demonstrate extraordinary flashes of unselfishness (realm of heavenly beings). These realms are neither merely psychological nor purely physical states, but they are felt realities in our everyday life. This aimless wandering through the six realms may go on indefinitely; hence it is called the infinite finitude of samsara.

Since samsara is the field of compassionate activity, the Buddha appears in the midst of the six realms. In graphic depictions of the six realms, for example, we find the Buddha situated at the very center of the wheel of samsara. He sits, surrounded by a pigeon, snake, and pig symbolizing greed, hatred, and ignorance, respectively. These so-called three poisons conceal the Buddha and cause the cycle of samsara to revolve endlessly. In some other drawings a Buddha stands in the middle of each of the six realms, ready to deliver beings no matter where they are located. Once again we are shown that the Buddha exists in the very midst of our delusory life, even awaiting us in the pit of hell. In either case, no matter where we are or what we are doing, the Buddha has already fulfilled the vow to deliver us from samsara.

Shinran had been a monk at the Tendai monastery atop Mt. Hiei for twenty years. Since the age of nine, he had undergone strict discipline, mastered the scriptures, and immersed himself in a variety of religious practices—meditating, visualizing, chanting, circumambulating, and so on. Yet he failed to have any kind of liberating experience. His failure only highlighted the darkness of ignorance within himself. He could not contain the demons within, and no existing practices could quiet his spiritual agitations. Since no one else could be faulted except himself, he concluded, "Hell is my only home."

The path of nembutsu, however, had been readied for Shinran and all those living in the age of *mappo*, the endtime of history, when not a single being attained enlightenment. This meant that delusion was no longer personal or psychological; it was historical and universal. But such a hopeless age was the opportune moment for the Pure Land path to emerge as the way of liberation for all people. It was welcomed, above all, by those who realized that no existing religious practice could meet their deep spiritual hunger. This new path received a radical formulation by Shinran that struck a responsive chord among earnest seekers:

Even a good person attains birth in the Pure Land, how much more so the evil person. . . . The Primal Vow was established out of deep compassion for us who cannot become freed from the bondage of birth-and-death through any religious practice, due to the abundance of blind passions. Since its basic intention is to effect the enlightenment of such an evil one, the evil person who entrusts the self to Other Power is truly the one who

attains birth in the Pure Land. Thus, even the good
person attains birth, how much more so the evil person!
(*Tannisho* III)

According to Shinran, however, the Pure Land teaching was rele-
vant for the people not only in the latter age of decline but in all
periods of history, simply because the limitation of karmic beings is universal, being consistent throughout history. Thus, the
working of the Primal Vow is directed not only to sentient
beings in a specific period but in all ages past, present, and
future. Shinran states this clearly:

> In the three periods of True, Simulated,
>   and Corrupt Dharma
> The Primal Vow of Amida prevails
> In our age of Simulated and Corrupt Dharma
> All good practices have entered the Palace of Dragons.

While the Primal Vow was meant for all periods, the bankruptcy of traditional practices was required for it to emerge on
the center stage of history.

The presence of the Buddha in the bottom of hell is central
to Shinran's assertion that "Even a good person attains birth in
the Pure Land, how much more so the evil person." Once at a
Shin temple the congregation was asked by the priest, "How
many of you are positive of going to hell?" Only one hand went
up. And then he asked, "How many of you are positive of going
to the Pure Land?" Again, only one hand went up. Both hands
belonged to Genza. Through the accumulation of deep hearing,
Genza knew that he was destined for hell, but at the same time
he rejoiced in the Primal Vow directed to such a being of karmic
evil like himself. The being destined for hell is the same person

destined to be born in the Pure Land by virtue of true compassion. The empty bucket lowered into the deep well is the same bucket lifted up, now filled with water.

Such a transformation is beyond ordinary comprehension. In fact, the power of reason, always focused on externals, fails to see the karmic evil within and its ultimate transformation. Reason alone cannot appreciate the paradoxical truth at the heart of true liberation. One of the chief characteristics of the emerging Buddhism in America has been the avoidance of the problem of evil. As one observer remarked, people in the West become absorbed in "therapeutic Buddhism," while in Asia it is "faith Buddhism." The goal of therapy is a healthy, happy, and productive life. That is fine, but that is only one half of the story of our life. Unless we grapple with the other half—evil, sin, suffering, and death—our story remains incomplete. We all need to seriously consider the words of the noted Jewish scholar Gershom Scholem: "To the intellect the problem [of evil] is no real problem at all. All that is needed is to understand that evil is relative, more, that it does not really exist . . . [but] the power of evil is real, and the mind which is conscious of this fact refuses to content itself with intellectual tours de force, however brilliant, which try to explain away the existence of something it knows to be there."

THE WORLD
OF DEW

33

When Buddhism was introduced into Japan in the mid-sixth century, it had an enormous impact, an impact that enriched and heightened the sensitivity to life, nature, and the world. As Earl Miner points out in *An Introduction to Japanese Court Poetry*, the Buddhist teaching of impermanence enhanced the sense of desolation and celebration found among the poets of the Heian Period (794–1185). One of the favorite metaphors for impermanence, flux, and change was dewdrops. It signified the fragile, fleeting nature of human life. An early example from this period is the following poem by Ki no Tomonori:

> What good is life?
> Is it really nothing more substantial
> Than the drying dew—
> I would exchange it without regret
> For just one night with her I love!

南無阿彌陀佛

In this early period the notion of impermanence had a negative tone, carrying a tinge of sadness, regret, pathos. But with the passing of time it took on a more positive tone, an encouragement to discover an enduring, unchanging reality beyond the phenomenal world. This is clearly found in the priest-poet Ryokan (1756–1831). He was a Zen monk imbued with Pure Land sensitivity who wrote several poems on Amida, such as the following:

> If not for Amida's inconceivable vow
> What then would remain to me
> As a keepsake of this world?

He encourages people to follow the path of nembutsu, the oft-quoted one being:

> Return to Amida,
> Return to Amida,
> So even dewdrops fall.

Everything in our evanescent world constantly reminds us not to rely on passing, unreliable things but to entrust ourselves to that which is timeless—Immeasurable Light and Life that is Amida.

Ryokan alerts us to the fact that when we encounter difficulties and failures, experience frustration and despair, they are all telling us, "Return to Amida, return to Amida." When our trust has been betrayed or our love unfulfilled, it tells us, "Return to Amida, return to Amida." When our bodies begin to deteriorate and bones start creaking, we are reminded again, "Return to Amida, return to Amida." When the slightest sign of illness causes fear and anxiety, the body is pleading, "Return to Amida, return to Amida." And when death approaches us, whether we

like it or not, we shall all "Return to Amida, return to Amida."
This is not an escape from the world but a discovery of our
roots in timeless reality. The return is twofold—returning to the
roots and then back again to everyday life—so that we can live
with some measure of wisdom and compassion.

Among the well-known poems referring to dew is the one by
Issa (1763–1828), the Shin priest-poet, whose many haiku celebrate insignificant creatures—fleas, frogs, snakes, and fireflies—
as well as little children, peasants, and woodcutters. Belonging to
the Shin tradition that approved a married clergy since the thirteenth century, Issa got married late in his life and had three
children. All three died before they reached the age of one.
When he lost his third child, a daughter, he expressed his grief
and sorrow:

> The world of dew
> Is the world of dew
> And yet, and yet . . .

Once at a Buddhist-Christian dialogue conference, my counter-
part quoted this poem as evidence that Issa had not yet attained
enlightenment. The last line showed that he was unable to accept the truth of impermanence manifested in his daughter's
death. From a dualistic point of view that differentiates attachment from nonattachment, this professor's interpretation may
appear to be valid.

From a nondualistic viewpoint, however, the opposite is the
case: *because* Issa was a fully awakened human being, he could be
himself thoroughly—grasping, longing, and deeply attached to
his loved one. His sorrow over the loss of his beloved daughter
exceeds the bounds of commonsense understanding. Instead of
trying to cover up, suppress, or transcend grief—all calculative

maneuvers—Issa could be his completely foolish self within the boundless compassion of the Buddha. Nonattachment comes alive only by working through attachment; otherwise, nonattachment by itself becomes just another human construct, another object of attachment.

In the first two lines Issa completely agrees with the truth of impermanence. Yes, he is saying, this world of dew is the world of dew; there is no question about it. But that is a philosophical proposition. When it comes to his own daughter's death, Issa says, I can't let go, I can't forget—"and yet and yet." Within the boundless space provided by true compassion, Issa cannot help but be his grieving human self. In this liberation not only Issa but his daughter, too, come really alive, transcending time and space.

Whenever I think of the dew metaphor, I recall a verse by Percy Bysshe Shelley in "Hellas" from my school days:

> Worlds on worlds are rolling ever
> From creation to decay,
> Like bubbles on a river,
> Sparkling, bursting, borne away.

Our life is short and momentary, like bubbles on a river. For this reason Shin Buddhists celebrate and treasure each sparkling moment, all the more precious because it will soon vanish and disappear. But life, "bursting, borne away," is also reality that is to be affirmed and treasured.

UNREPEATABLE LIFE

34

南無阿彌陀佛

Traditionally, people have sought the Buddhist religious life for either of two basic reasons. First is the powerful sense of life's fragility and impermanence—if all is passing, what is the significance of human existence? Second is the profound awareness as a karmic being—if one is limited, imperfect, and finite, how can we ever achieve true peace and fulfillment? The two may be different but are interrelated, for affirming impermanence is the same thing as accepting human finitude. Thus, whichever question one pursues, the answer comes down to this: cherish this unrepeatable life by living fully and gratefully each moment of our finite existence. This is the point of departure that evolves without limits into the life of wisdom and compassion.

Stories of such a way of life exist in abundance in the Shin tradition, but we will look at one exemplary case. A devout Shin Buddhist,

Mrs. K. Takeuchi, a housewife, suffered terminal cancer and
passed away in 1965 at the age of forty-six. I did not know her
personally but became acquainted with her through her poems
given to me by a mutual friend.

Mrs. Takeuchi underwent several operations for brain tumor.
After her last operation, she composed the following poem on
her hospital bed:

> Listen to the call of the Primal Vow,
> So life granted me to this day,
> For shallow is my appreciation
> Of true and real life sustaining me.

The reprieve of a single day contains infinite significance—she is
given another opportunity to savor the call of Immeasurable
Light and Immeasurable Life. But her illness and the repeated
surgeries must have taken its toll. Especially was this so, whenever she thought of her family, the poor prognosis of recovery,
and the accumulating financial burden.

No one, she realized, can be blamed for her condition. She
must endure the consequences of her karmic life. But, of course,
she is not alone, left to her fate. She writes:

> Faint is my own strength
> To carry the weight of my karmic destiny,
> But strength and power infuse me
> In the saying of namu-amida-butsu.

Having devoted her life to the interior practice of deep hearing,
Mrs. Takeuchi had been made fully aware of great compassion,
focusing on a karma-bound person like herself and working
ceaselessly to emancipate her from suffering.

But now in her last moments, racked with pain and facing imminent death, everything vanished like the spring snow. In the very abyss of despair, she again experienced a lightness of being, for she was made aware of how truly blessed she was:

> I know not karmic evil,
> I know not gratitude,
> But on this self showers
> All the compassion of countless universes.

When her conscious awareness of gratitude vanished, all the more the compassion of countless universes showered upon her. It gave her renewed strength and peace in her final hours. In Buddhist lore references are made to countless universes, since there can be only one Buddha in a given realm. Sakyamuni Buddha appears in our samsaric world, other Buddhas exist in their respective realms, and Amida Buddha presides over the Western Pure Land.

Astronomers tell us that billions of universes like ours may exist in the cosmos. While Buddhist thinkers had no scientific evidence, they constantly spoke of innumerable universes. Boundless compassion, permeating each of these universes, spills over into the cosmos. At the center of this flood of compassion lies Mrs. Takeuchi in her sickbed, receiving the sustenance and prayers of countless Buddhas. No need to know karmic evil, no need to feel gratitude, just the nembutsu acknowledging her life now approaching consummation, birth in the Pure Land.

For Mrs. Takeuchi each day on the horizontal plane was sustained by the power of the Primal Vow coming from the deep center of life. This enabled her to live out her life with dignity and quiet joy.

This day,
Endowed with true and real life,
Will never be repeated in eternity—
How precious this single day!

I remember once reading about the infinitesimal chance of being born into human life. A scientist calculated that it is comparable to rolling a six in dice five million times in succession. Not five hundred times, not even five thousand times, but five million times in succession! As intelligent, thinking people, how can we not ask, What is the significance of this human life? Whence do I come? Whither do I go? The Buddhist tradition makes the same point by recourse to the metaphor of the blind turtle and the floating yoke.

The Buddha speaks to a group of his disciples about a yoke with a hole floating in the ocean. It keeps moving in the direction of the wind, bobbing up and down with the waves. A wind from the east takes it westward, a wind from the west pushes it eastward, a wind from the north moves it southward, a wind from the south shifts it northward. In this great ocean also lives a blind turtle who comes to the surface once every hundred years. The Buddha asks his disciples:

What chance does this turtle have of pushing his head through the hole in the yoke? . . . Sooner or later, monks, a blind turtle will push his head through the hole in a yoke; but more difficult than that is to be born into human life.

Although Mrs. Takeuchi suffered in her illness, she had realized the full significance of having been born into human life. Awakening to the Buddha Dharma, her body was permeated with Light and Life. She thus became liberated forever from the aimless cycle of existence. One of her final poems expresses her profound gratitude to the priceless gift of this unrepeatable life:

In this life
No end to comparing myself
To those above and to those below.

Half of my body paralyzed,
Still I have my right hand, my ears, my right leg.
Although with brain tumor,
Still there exist taste, color, sound, voice, words, smell.

But they too will soon be no more
As my body will be no more;
But the nembutsu, Amida, true compassion, Pure
      Land
Will always remain.

How fortunate am I, How happy am I,
Now and forevermore.

Although Mrs. Takeuchi ended her mortal life on earth, she continues to live today affecting everyone who remembers her words. What she accomplished in her short existence on earth is an inspiration to all who have heard her story. The ripple effects of her life continue to expand ever more among those of us who see her as a living embodiment of the nembutsu.

Mrs. Takeuchi's life is summed up by Saichi in his typically succinct and direct manner:

How grateful!
While others die,
I do not die;
Not dying, I go
To Amida's Pure Land

It is easy to talk about life as being precious and unrepeatable, but unless we truly know the reason, the words can be empty and hollow. Only by being awakened by the timeless working of true compassion can we fully appreciate each living instant as filled with infinite worth. Such an awesome reverence for life must become the basis of a new ethic in order to effectively cope with the manifold, complex problems facing the world today.

MY GRANDMOTHER

35

南無阿彌陀佛

I have been very fortunate in my life. Due to various good karmic strands coming together, I have been able to study with eminent scholars of Buddhism and have encountered many Shin teachers and lay men and women who shared with me the gift of nembutsu. Adding immensely to my world of understanding are all kinds of friends from various religious and philosophical persuasions—wise, thoughtful, cynical, brusque, humorous—from whom I have learned much. But the greatest impact on my spiritual life has been my grandmother who died at the age of eighty-six in 1964.

A simple and unaffected woman, "namu-amida-butsu" came spilling out of her mouth, like little Buddhas competing to get out of her tiny body that could not contain the joy she felt of having been embraced by Immeasurable Light and Immeasurable Life. Hers was not an easy life, but she lived it with spiritual exuberance and vigor.

My grandfather was the twelfth generation priest of a Shin temple in Fukuoka. A vigorous man with a fiery temper and a booming voice, he was nicknamed *kaminari,* "thunder and lightning." My grandmother was his third wife, a fact she was to discover after they got married. The first two, unable to stand my demanding grandfather, just ran away.

The first relative that my grandmother met, when she made a round of courtesy calls, was his aunt. Her opening remark was not a cordial greeting but a challenge: "Have you settled the matter of the afterlife?" This was a common question posed to Shin followers. It is asking whether one has successfully resolved the question of death and dying. The answer reveals the degree to which a person has realized the Buddha Dharma and, consequently, appreciates the meaning of this life. The Zen equivalent would be the koan: "What is your original face before you were born of father and mother?"

My grandmother was taken aback by the totally unexpected greeting. She froze, unable to say a word. But later she was determined to find an answer. It was not easy for a young housewife, maintaining a large household, cooking three meals a day, catering to the demands of my grandfather, meeting the social needs of a temple wife, and eventually bearing five children. In order to find time for the Buddha Dharma, she would sneak out of the house early in the morning before sunrise and before my grandfather woke up. She then would go to a famous Shin temple, Manpukuji, where daily morning services were held at 6 A.M. She would participate in chanting, dharma talks, and question-answer periods. When the session concluded, my grandmother would run home and prepare breakfast for the family before they got up. This, of course, was years before the convenience of electricity, gas, and running hot water.

My mother remembers as a pre-schooler when she and her younger brother were taken to these early morning services, bundled up by my grandmother on cold winter mornings and sitting in a temple through freezing temperature. When the service ended, they would dash home before my grandfather came down for breakfast. They were always afraid of what might happen if he ever found out. She lived the advice of one of her favorite teachers, Daiei Kaneko: "Receive material gifts with your heart; receive the Buddha Dharma with your body." My grandmother engaged in deep hearing using both her body and mind, walking daily to attend temple services in the early morning hours and never accepting anything without relentless and thorough questioning.

Having resolved the question of death and dying in the middle of her life, grandmother lived the nembutsu. Her every movement expressed deep joy and appreciation. When she sat down, she would say, "namu-amida-butsu." When she stood up, "namu-amida-butsu." When she sipped a cup of tea, "namu-amida-butsu," and when she finished, "namu-amida-butsu." When she greeted guests, before any formality, "namu-amida-butsu." When she said good-bye, "namu-amida-butsu." She lived out Shan-tao's exhortation that had a decisive impact on the founding of the new Pure Land school by Honen in 1175:

Repeat the nembutsu with a single-hearted devotion, whether walking, standing, sitting, or lying down, without question of the length of time, never ceasing for a single moment. This is truly the ultimate practice which without fail results in emancipation, for it accords with the Primal Vow of Amida Buddha.

But she was not the stereotypical pious follower. I remember visiting her one winter in Fukuoka, when she got very upset and angry at a visitor. My grandmother and I were seated around a charcoal brazier, keeping our hands warm, when someone came to the entrance door. My grandmother stood up and went to the door. Although I could not see the two, I heard my grandmother arguing with an elderly man, both shouting and yelling at each other. Soon I heard the door slam shut, and my grandmother came back, huffing and puffing. She was very, very upset.

When I asked her what happened, she glared at me, saying, "That scoundrel goes around fooling old folks, swindling their money, and thinks nothing of it. That beast, he gets me so angry!" Immediately following this flowed out the nembutsu, "namu-amida-butsu, namu-amida-butsu." To call someone a "beast" is our equivalent of shouting S.O.B. This is the worst thing one can say of another in the Japanese vernacular. It refers to a person being subhuman, one of the lower realms of the wheel of transmigration. Unlike the English language, spoken Japanese has no profanity and almost no obscenity; therefore, to call another person a beast is the harshest opprobrium.

My grandmother's fiery temper almost exploded but was immediately defused by the nembutsu. Boundless compassion permitted her to manifest her karmic passions but immediately extinguished the erupting anger. If sudden transformation had not occurred, the situation could have invited dire consequences. Following this incident, she immediately took concrete steps, informed the authorities about the scam artist, and mobilized other victims in order to get him arrested.

My grandmother died a natural death at the age of eighty-six, her body weakening and her senses declining, but her mind was sharp and clear to the very end. I asked my spinster aunt who took care of her to write down any thoughts that my

grandmother might express in her last moments. About a week
before she passed away, my aunt tried to comfort her by saying,
"Grandma, when you leave this world, I'm going to be left all
alone, but you're fortunate, because you'll be going to the Pure
Land where you'll see Grandpa, your sister, all your old friends!"
Lying in bed, Grandmother replied, "No, no! There's no such
place called Pure Land . . . namu-amida-butsu, namu-amida-
butsu."

For my grandmother there was no separation between this
temporal world of samsara and the timeless life that is the Pure
Land. Her "no, no" negated the Pure Land as an object of
dualistic thinking, but her saying of nembutsu affirmed the Pure
Land here and now, the here and now "both in and out of time."
Saichi would have fully agreed with my grandmother:

> O Saichi, where is the Land of Bliss?
> My Land of Bliss is right here.
> Where is the line of division?
> Between this world and the Land of Bliss?
> The eyes are the line of division.

Having been touched and blessed by Immeasurable Light and
Immeasurable Life, my grandmother lived a full and rich life.
While being a person karma-bound, she relished the life of
unbounded freedom. With Saichi she could sing:

> Although my defiled body remains unchanged,
> By the tireless working of Amida's compassion
> My self-power turned into Other Power,
> I play in the Pure Land of Amida.

THE PURE LAND

36

In contrast to our world of delusion exists the world of enlightenment. The world of delusion is created by karma-bound beings, entangled in scheming and calculating gains and losses that constitute our daily pursuit. The world of enlightenment is the realm of wisdom and compassion of fully awakened beings, liberated from all egocentric impulses. This is the Pure Land, presided over by the Buddha of Immeasurable Light and Life. It cannot be seen by persons who are not attuned to the religious life.

The Pure Land defies our conventional understanding, because it is not an object of dualistic knowing. It does not exist, for example, like Hawaii, the paradise of the Pacific, in the middle of an ocean. But it can be appreciated fully when our religious quest evolves and matures, free of discursive rhetoric and conceptualized notions regarding reality.

南無阿彌陀佛

To clarify what this means, we turn to Shinran's understanding of the Buddha and Pure Land. He writes:

The Buddha is the Tathagata of Inconceivable Light and
the Pure Land is the land of Immeasurable Light.

Shinran here is not referring to an objective being called Amida Buddha or to a geographical place called the Pure Land, each emitting rays of light. Rather, he is saying that wherever the illumination of Light occurs, wherever religious sensitivity and consciousness are raised, there the reality of Amida and Pure Land comes to the fore.

We normally think that our eyes make sight possible. That is true, but in the darkness we cannot see anything, even if we have sight. It is by virtue of light that we are able to see things. In the same way, it is by the illumination of Immeasurable Light that we come to see our true reality—a foolish being of karmic evil. Such an awareness is born not because we are wise but because of wisdom that touches us in the "form" of Light.

When one is thus illuminated and touched, an intimate relationship with Light occurs, and Amida and Pure Land are appreciated as the concrete manifestation of a transcendent reality. This reality is called *dharmakaya-as-suchness*, which is formless and nameless. From this formless and nameless reality appears *dharmakaya-as-compassion* in the form of Amida and Pure Land. Thus, we are able to encounter transcendent reality in the midst of our samsaric life. Before proceeding further, let us briefly note the evolution of the idea of Pure Land that was understood variously in different historical epochs.

The term "Pure Land" is a translation from the Chinese *ching-t'u* (*Jodo* in Japanese). It does not exist in Sanskrit Buddhist literature. The closest equivalent in Sanskrit would be the phrase "purification of the Buddha land." Abundant references to countless Pure Lands are found in Chinese Buddhist literature from the first century C.E. Various Buddhas in the Mahayana pantheon reside over purified lands, but it is the Pure Land of Amida that comes to be significant in East Asia.

As the idea of Pure Land evolved, it was first seen as the ideal environment conducive to religious discipline and spiritual progress. Freed from the cacophony of worldly temptations, one could progress uninterrupted on the path of enlightenment to attain Buddhahood. Although variations in the notion of Pure Land appear subsequently, it becomes the ultimate goal of the highest religious aspiration.

One of the most influential works on the Pure Land in Japanese Buddhism is *The Essentials of Birth* by the Tendai monk Genshin, who lived in the late tenth century. He formed an exclusive religious society, consisting of members from the upper classes, to promote contemplation and visualization of the Pure Land. Their ultimate aim was to receive the welcome by Amida at death, attain birth on a lotus flower in the Pure Land, and acquire the thirty-two marks of a great being. The Pure Land is rich with images symbolizing the awakened or enlightened state: singing birds, celestial music, beautiful flowers, radiant light, fragrant aroma, bejeweled streams, trees covered with bells, heavenly musical instruments playing. In this realm one is assured of eternal life, union with loved ones and friends, hearing Amida's preaching, and making offerings to the Buddha.

During this period, a deathbed ritual that guaranteed birth in the Pure Land became popular. A painted screen with the figure of Amida, looking down from among mountain peaks, would be placed at the head of a deathbed. The dying person would grasp a string connected to the screen, so that birth in the Pure Land would be assured. Surrounded by family, friends, and the faithful, one receives a grand send-off from this world of samsara and a warm welcome by Amida in the Pure Land.

This view of Amida and Pure Land undergoes a major change in the twelfth century, especially in the thought of Honen and Shinran. The gradual transformation, for example, is already reflected in the visual arts. In contrast to earlier depictions showing Amida in a seated position and welcoming the dead to the Pure Land, the later paintings portray Amida standing on a cloud, streaking down into the world to save all beings.

The latter culminates in Shinran's radical reinterpretation of "birth in the Pure Land" in two ways. First, he sees "birth" as a synonym for liberation attainable here and now, while remaining in karmic bondage. When one completely entrusts the self to Amida, birth is attained, according to Shinran, "immediately; immediately means without any passage of time, without any passage of days." Since the Pure Land transcends time and space, it appears not only in the future but in this very present.

Second, birth in the Pure Land means simultaneous attainment of Buddhahood. At the moment of death one is freed of all karmic indebtedness. This is birth in the Pure Land that is simultaneously the ultimate liberation: attainment of Buddhahood. Unlike the traditional view that required a long period of training in the Pure Land before attaining Buddhahood, Shinran affirmed supreme enlightenment at the moment of death by virtue of the working of great compassion.

Furthermore, since perfect enlightenment is attained in the Pure Land, one returns immediately to samsara for the salvation of all beings. Self-enlightenment is conditional on the enlightenment of others. Thus, the Pure Land is not the final destination; it is a way station on the return trip to samsara. The basic paradigm is the Mahayana bodhisattva who strives for enlightenment (ascent) for the sake of engaging in salvific activity (descent). Shinran calls this ascent *oso-eko*, going to the Pure Land by the power endowed by great compassion, and he calls descent *genso-eko*, returning from the Pure Land by the selfsame power of compassion.

The Pure Land as a way station reminds me of a Hasidic story retold by Martin Buber. On one of the days of the Hanukkah feast, it is said, Rabbi Nahum found his disciples playing checkers. They were embarrassed, but the Rabbi asked whether they were aware of the rules of the game. When no one answered, he is said to have explained the game as follows. The first is that one must not make two moves at once. The second is that one may only move forward and not backward. And the third is that when one has reached the last row, one may move wherever one likes.

The main point of this story is that single-minded commitment is essential for the religious life before one attains the freedom to do whatever the heart desires. The first and second moves are the ascent; the third move is the descent. When one has reached the goal, "the last row," the person is empowered to move about freely without any restrictions or boundaries. Having realized the fullest measure of wisdom and compassion by "birth in the Pure Land," one is now free to work for the liberation of all beings.

The ultimate goal of a Shin Buddhist is not personal salvation but the deliverance of all beings from samsara. The model is the life of the historical Buddha. In the words of Shinran:

> Those who attain the Pure Land of peace
> Return to this world of five defilements,
> And like Sakyamuni Buddha
> Bring endless benefits to all beings.

WHEN A PERSON DIES

37

What happens when a person dies? Where does he or she go? Is there something that lives on forever? What is the meaning of death and dying? These questions are frequently asked by people, whether religious or not. Buddhists take these questions seriously, for the answers to such questions have direct bearing on how we live this unrepeatable life.

Buddhism encourages people to face death and dying squarely in order to awaken to a reality more elemental than life and death. Rather than being an obsession with death, it provides an opening to appreciate and celebrate true and real life. Thus, Buddhist funerals and memorial services are observed for the sake of the living, just as much as it is for the dead. It provides another solemn occasion for the deep hearing of the Buddha Dharma. The question of death necessarily engages our whole being with the meaning of life.

A few years ago a terrible tragedy occurred in my hometown. A young mother and her little son were brutally murdered by the father of the boy. This devastated the family and shocked the community. The little boy's grandmother was especially pained, and some time later she asked me what happens to people when they die. Her questioning was not religiously motivated, so I tried my best to give a tentative answer that she could understand but still prompt her to take up the religious quest.

I live in the woods on the outskirts of the city, so occasionally we have field mice getting into our attic. Sometimes when I sit quietly in my study, I can hear the mice playing soccer in the ceiling. I sit there wondering what's going on, but I can't see through the ceiling and know what is there. I eat three meals a day, but I'm ignorant of what's happening in my stomach, kidney, liver, gall bladder. I drive my car to work daily, but I really don't know what's going on under the hood of the car. I live in a comfortable house, but without electricity, as recently happened, I wouldn't know what to do. My mother is eighty-eight years old, very alert with a keen mind, but I can't fathom her thoughts or feelings.

This inability to know extends to metaphysical truths. In the famous parable of the poison arrow found in early Buddhism, a young monk, Malunkyaputta, is unhappy because the Buddha refuses to answer metaphysical questions. They include fourteen unanswerable questions, such as whether the universe is finite or not, whether the world is eternal or not, whether a saint lives after death or not, and so forth.

The Buddha informs the monk that his teaching does not deal with metaphysical questions, because his Middle Path is a practical one meant to solve the immediate problems of living. He then gives a parable. The Buddha asks, If you were walking in the forest and got shot by a poison arrow, what would you do? Would you have the arrow extracted immediately, or would you first ask questions and demand answers before doing anything? Endless questions may arise—who shot the arrow, where did he come from, to what clan did he belong, what did he look like, who made the poison?

The sensible thing is to have the poison arrow immediately removed and let the healing process begin. The Buddha's teaching is meant to confront practical, everyday problems and find workable solutions. It is not concerned with questions that cannot be verified by experience. The question of death and dying is also approached in the same way.

First, our inability to know what happens to a person after death is decisive proof of our limited intellect. This forces us to examine our own life. When we do so, we confront our own finitude—that we will not live forever. We then begin to ask some fundamental questions neglected in everyday life: Who am I, for what purpose am I living, where does life come from, where does it go?

Second, as we struggle for understanding, we are made keenly aware that some problems in both life and death may have no answers. If that is the case, our task is to cherish this living moment, take good care of our bodies, open our hearts and minds to others, treasure friendships, and live fully here and now. As we do so, we come to see death in a different light. Death does not threaten us from the outside; it has always been within us since birth. We come to see that both living and dying are manifestations of a natural process. As we awaken to this fact, our apprehensions about death and dying slowly become transformed into a deeper appreciation for this life.

Third, since such an appreciation is beyond reason or logic or conventional thinking, it cannot be comprehended by the small-minded self alone. But when we awaken, touched by the

Light of compassion, we come to see it clearly. Bountiful life has always been here with us, but we rarely recognize it because our attention is misdirected. Our life is made possible by the gifts of air, sunshine, and water, yet we hardly give thought to them and even less show gratitude to them. Now, boundless compassion permeates not only our life but also our death; it permeates the seen and unseen universes; it courses through both our living and our dying. The Zen master Dogen puts it precisely: "Life is the manifestation of the total dynamic working; death is the manifestation of total dynamic working."

All this is contained in the Name-that-calls, the sounding of "namu-amida-butsu." No matter who, what, or where, whether living or dying, each of us is *namu,* inseparably bound to the dynamic life that is *amida-butsu.* Thus, wherever "namu-amida-butsu" is intoned, all beings both in life and in death come truly alive for the first time. The division between living and dying is overcome by the Name-that-calls.

My burning question when my friend took his own life was, Is my friend happy now? But with the passing of years I realize that as human beings, wandering in the darkness of ignorance, we can never know what is beyond this life. We cannot even know the most obvious things—other people's minds, what goes on in the room beyond the wall, what awaits us in the next instant of life. This inability to know everything is the very definition of what it means to be human. Yet, without truly knowing ourselves as such we can never be satisfied with material or social achievements, and we can never know what true fulfillment is.

Having been illuminated, even if faintly, to the reality of my self-delusion, I come to see myself as the object of boundless compassion. But I see not only myself—I also see my friend Teruo as the ultimate concern of great compassion. But, as the years pass, he is more than that, for I come to see him more and more as a bodhisattva who comes from the vortex of boundless compassion to guide me into the universe of true and real life.

Whenever I think of my departed friend, I am reminded of the poem that has been handed down among Shin Buddhists. In fondly remembering our loved ones, we hear their entreating call:

> If you miss me,
> Say namu-amida-butsu
> For I, too, live
> In the six letters.

The nembutsu is not a mindless phrase but a grand affirmation of life in which we discover that both living and dying contain infinite significance. In such an appreciation we gain new strength and courage to live each moment fully and gratefully, extending compassion to all beings without end.

HOUSE OR HOME

38

A house, according to the dictionary, is a structure having a specific function, primarily serving as a dwelling for one or more families. A home, on the other hand, is not just a building or structure but a domicile of family ties and domestic comfort. It is a place of rest, normally filled with love, warmth, and laughter. The difference between a house and a home is not a simple matter, for some houses with people living in them may be empty and cold, while other houses with a single occupant may be filled with intangible warmth.

The significant difference between a house and a home may be found in the rich variety of compounds relating positively to home in everyday usage. We say, for example, "I feel at home," to suggest a feeling of ease and comfort even in unfamiliar settings. "Being at home" suggests familiarity with a foreign language, new tool, or complicated skill. Home is very desirable in athletics: home base, home ground, home game, home run, and home free. Nostalgia is invoked by the words hometown, homeland, home range, homespun, homecoming. Wholesome, tasty food is suggested by homemade, home baked, and home cooking. Such phrases as "the arrow struck home" and "it struck home" have a powerful impact.

I find a parallel to house and home in human beings. When we think of ourselves primarily in terms of physical or external attributes, it's like talking about a house. But when we see ourselves as embodying a richer life within, especially the spiritual, it gives the feeling of a home. In this analogy the body is like a container (house) in which flows true and real life (home). This vital life is religiously called Immeasurable Light and Life.

The goal of the Buddhist path is to awaken to the true and real life that flows within us. But this life is inseparable from the physical container. Thus, when the two are fully integrated through self-cultivation and religious practice, both mind and body become supple, pliant, and open. This is contrasted to ordinary thinking that divides mind and body, creating an imbalance between the two, resulting in a rigid mind and a tense body. The current fashion for Yoga exercise may contribute to a healthy body, but its true significance is realized only when it is pursued as part of an integrated Hindu spiritual practice.

Since most of us neglect or ignore the true and real life that flows through us, it calls attention to itself through the Name, "namu-amida-butsu." In our saying of namu-amida-butsu, it is actually life calling unto life itself, whether people are aware of it or not. When we respond fully to this call, we shed the self-enclosure of the ego-self and return to the freedom of true and real life. The Shin teacher Daiei Kaneko expressed this graphically, "The saying of nembutsu is the sound of the disintegrating ego, and the labor pains of a new self being born."

Namu-amida-butsu affirms one's fundamental nature as true and real life. The isolated, wandering, and insecure *namu* has finally come home to *amida-butsu*. The arrival celebrates both rest and renewal. Saichi writes:

> Namu-amida-butsu
> Is like the moon, like the sun;
> It is like the rising sun.
> My mind grows warm, so does the body.
> Let me take a rest for a while here.
> Namu-amida-butsu. Namu-amida-butsu.

Since one has arrived home, nothing is required. One simply takes utmost care of one's given body, since without it the awakening to dynamic life would have been impossible, and one acts compassionately in the world as the most natural and spontaneous way of life. The person of nembutsu is always at home, no matter where or what one may be doing. No conditions are attached, not even the saying of nembutsu.

> I don't say any nembutsu.
> It isn't necessary.
> Saved by the Buddha's compassion,
> How grateful I am.
> Namu-amida-butsu is ever with me,
> And I am ever with it.
> While asleep, namu-amida-butsu.
> While awake, namu-amida-butsu.
> While walking, resting, sitting, or lying,
>   namu-amida-butsu.
> While working, namu-amida-butsu.

TRUE AND
REAL LIFE

39

In 1975 I taught at the University of Hawaii as a
visiting professor of philosophy and religion, and
simultaneously I was appointed as the Scholar-in-
Residence at the Buddhist Study Center (BSC)
located near the campus. BSC is part of the Shin
Buddhist organization known as the Honpa
Hongwanji Mission of Hawaii. At this center I
gave weekly lectures on Shin Buddhism to a general audience reflecting the multiethnic makeup
of the community. Among the regular partici-
pants was a Caucasian woman who came to participate from Wahiawa, a small town in Oahu,
about a forty-five-minute drive from the Center.

One day she asked me to visit her mother in
the Wahiawa General Hospital. The mother was
eighty-six years old, totally deaf, and absolutely
refusing to eat. This caused great distress and
anguish for the family, and they wondered
whether I could talk their mother into eating

again. On the day I had agreed to visit her, I had a heavy
schedule, so I had no time to prepare what I might say. I would
be meeting a complete stranger who was deaf and who had never
been exposed to Buddhism.

I was picked up and taken to the hospital where I was
introduced to the mother. Although gaunt, pale, and looking
weak, she struck me as the epitome of stubborn old age. When I
held her hands, however, a faint smile crossed her face; her
whispering was barely audible, but I understood that she had
been waiting for me.

I took the writing pad next to her bed and with a felt pen
wrote in large, bold letters, so the deaf woman could read them
easily:

> Your body is a container of life. It contains true and real
> life. Your body and your true and real life are two differ-
> ent things, related but different.

I tore off the sheet of paper and handed it to her. Then, I
immediately began writing on the second sheet of paper:

> Your body is old and tired and doesn't want to go on
> living anymore, but true and real life within you is not.
> In fact, it wants to live on forever.

Tearing off this sheet and handing it over to her, I continued
writing on eleven successive pages:

> You have taken care of your body up to now, but now
> you must take care of true and real life that flows within

you. Something deep within you wants you to awaken to the precious life that moves within you.

As you awaken to true and real life within you, you will feel good and warm and alive. Then everyone, including those who love you, will also awaken to that same true and real life.

Although I don't know you at all, in one sense I have always known you—through true and real life that flows in you and me and everyone around us. Because of this shared life, I love you deeply as I love myself deeply.

When we appreciate true and real life that flows in the deepest parts of ourselves, then we also take good care of its container, this body, for without it we could never have come to realize true and real life.

To die or not to die—we really don't have a choice. If we could choose, it would make things so simple. All we can do is to take good care of our body and our life, until the fullness of time and being brings to close our existence on this earth.

As the woman read each successive page slowly as it was passed on to her, she became more and more alert, and her eyes focused on each word.

In my own life I often forget about true and real life deep within me. But whenever I do and get lonely, unhappy, frustrated, or angry, something deep within me calls me to awaken to true and real life.

The call is a call for me to return to my real home, the home of homes, where all existence really comes alive. I hear the call through the words, namu-amida-butsu. This is known as the Name-that-calls.

Namu is me—lost, confused, and wanting to find my real home. Amida is Immeasurable Life and Light—true and real life which is my home of homes. Butsu is Buddha—the awakening to this true and real life. The three are not separate but one, so we say namu-amida-butsu.

In response to the Name-that-calls, I say namu-amida-butsu. This is my acceptance and affirmation of true and real life. No need to understand, no need to explain anything, no need to convince anyone. Just namu-amida-butsu.

Although I myself am incapable of truly loving another person, many people love me—many times in ways unknown to me. Although I fail to appreciate others' concern for me, they truly sustain my life. But when I live namu-amida-butsu, I am made to appreciate others and want to thank them—all this by virtue of true and real life.

I am then filled with warmth, love, and compassion. May you awaken to true and real life that flows in you, me, your loved ones, and all beings. Thank you for listening—not to me but to the call of true and real life coming from deep, deep within you and me.

Although I had a particularly heavy schedule that day—sitting meditation in early morning, meeting with students during the day, TV taping in the late afternoon, and preparing for the weekly *Tannisho* lecture that evening—the details have all but faded from my memory into the nebulous past. I learned later that she did begin eating again, but what remains with me is the gaunt yet hopeful face of the old woman, anticipating each sheet of paper.

BUDDHA-NATURE

40

I once heard an eminent Zen master say that even
Hitler had Buddha-nature but unfortunately it
was never manifested. This may be valid from the
Mahayana viewpoint, but Shinran would dis-
agree. Because of his realistic grasp of the limited,
foolish, and defiled nature of man, he saw even
himself as completely lacking in Buddha-nature.
What does this mean in the context of the
universality of Buddha-nature?

The Shin position is that Buddha-nature is
not a given, nor is it an abstract doctrine. The
same holds true for the mind that aspires for
enlightenment (*bodhicitta*). It too is virtually non-
existent in the average person. Shinran states his
understanding in the following verse:

> Karmic evil originally has no form;
> It comes from delusions and inverted
>   thinking;

The nature of Mind is originally pure,
But no one has a mind true and sincere.

Although "no one has a mind true and sincere," once a person is
awakened by the light of true compassion, the aspiration for
enlightenment becomes vividly real and Buddha-nature for the
first time becomes a dynamic reality.

All this, however, is contingent upon true entrusting that is
Amida's working being manifested in our life. True entrusting is
impossible coming from a karma-bound human being; it becomes true and real by virtue of great compassion, the all-
pervasive working of Tathagata that permeates the world. In
Shinran's formulation:

> Buddha-nature is none other than Tathagata. This
> Tathagata pervades the countless worlds; it fills the
> hearts and minds of the ocean of all beings. Thus, plants,
> trees, and land all attain Buddhahood. Since it is with
> this heart of mind of all sentient beings that they entrust
> themselves to the Vow of dharmakaya-as-compassion,
> this entrusting is none other than Buddha-nature.

When we entrust ourselves to Amida Buddha, it is Buddha-
nature appearing concretely in our lives. When Shinran equates
true entrusting with supreme enlightenment, Buddha or Tathagata, he is not saying that they are identical. Rather, he suggests
that the content of true entrusting, coming from the Buddha,
makes the person of true entrusting "equal" to the Buddha. This
ultimate realization is summed up by Shinran:

> The person who rejoices in true entrusting
> Is the equal of Tathagata;

True entrusting is Buddha-nature,
Buddha-nature is Tathagata.

Shinran's view of Buddha-nature ultimately accords with general
Mahayana thought but has a pragmatic quality. We can broaden
his experiential understanding within the scheme of thought
known as the "matrix of Tathagata" (*Tathagata-garbha*). This term
has two connotations. First, contained in each of us is a matrix
or womb (*garbha*) that has the potential of giving birth to Tathagata. And second, at the same time, each of us is contained
within the matrix or womb of the Tathagata. In Pure Land
vocabulary each of us is contained within the great compassion
of the Buddha Amida, and when this compassion is awakened in
us, Buddha-nature becomes a reality. Amida implants Buddha-
nature in us.

We can find different models of this twofold nature in world
religions, but a provocative contemporary formulation is the
"mythosphere" coined by Alexander Eliot. In his latest work, *The
Global Myth*, Eliot writes that the mythosphere

> resembles the refulgent dome of night by full moonlight,
> and yet at the same time it's more or less contiguous
> with our personal craniums. So we could say that it's
> inside our skins. On the other hand, we sometimes find
> ourselves in the mythosphere! Lacking its tumultuously
> fruitful influence, our mental lives would be almost as
> barren as the moon.

The mythosphere is the boundless compassion of the Buddha
that enfolds the universe, but it is also realized within each of us
as Buddha-nature. Our task in life is to awaken to the depth,
breadth, and richness of the mythosphere.

MOTHER TERESA
AND HITLER

41

A few years ago at Smith College there was a crisis, involving Hindu and Jewish students. The South Asian students put up posters with the swastika on it, announcing the Festival of Lights in the middle of November. Known as Divali, it is one of the holiest of Hindu observances. This offended the Jewish students who were observing Kristallnacht at the same time. Kristallnacht is a reminder of the reign of terror launched against the Jews in Germany and Austria on November 10, 1938. Mobs of people, incited by the Nazi government, destroyed 7,000 Jewish businesses, 267 synagogues, and sent thousands to concentration camps. This day of remembrance happened to coincide with the Hindu Festival of Lights.

The Jewish students saw the posters as the ultimate insult against their people and their faith. They demanded that the Hindu students

take down all the posters. The Hindu students adamantly refused, the swastika being the sacred symbol of Hinduism. They
accused the Jews of intolerance and bigotry. The students held
several meetings chaired by the Dean of the College in order to
reach a resolution to the conflict.

The Dean invited several faculty members, including myself,
to attend one of the last meetings. In preparation I made a quick
study of the history of the swastika and discovered its wide-
spread existence from prehistoric times in diverse civilizations.
This symbol of auspiciousness existed in Mohenjo-daro, Meso-
potamia, ancient Troy, Cyprus, Athens, Meso-america, central
Europe, Palestine, Italy, Scandinavia, Germany, and so on. It is
part of the Aryan legacy inherent in Indo-European cultures.
Hitler had appropriated it for his own use.

After a couple of hours of heated, emotionally charged debate among the students, we were asked to offer our views on
the subject. Speaking as a Buddhist, I told the students that I,
too, hold the swastika as a sacred symbol of my faith. It is found
on the earliest Buddhist art and architecture in India and South-
east Asia. Later it is carried to Tibet, China, Korea, Japan, and
other East Asian countries. The swastikas decorate the sacred
scriptures, mandalas, robes, funeral raiments, pillars, gates, and
sanctuaries of temples and monasteries. I could not help but
express my empathy with the Hindu students.

But as someone living in the twentieth century I also could
not ignore the Nazi genocide of millions of Jews, Poles, Com-
munists, Gypsies, homosexuals, and political prisoners during
World War II. In modern world history the swastika becomes
the ultimate symbol of evil. Thus, it is imperative that we recognize this German distortion of the swastika as containing a dark,
ominous power.

The impasse in the conflict had no rational solution satis-
factory to both sides. As an outsider, I could never fathom the
pain and terror experienced by the Jews under Nazi rule, nor
could I really feel the hurt and humiliation felt by the Hindu
students, far away from their homeland, being accused of insensitivity. But, I said, there is something that we can all do today,
regardless of where we come from. And that is to ask ourselves:
Have I always been free of bigotry and injustice? Have I always
treated others, whether individuals or groups with respect? Have
I always been free of insensitivity against those who are not like
us? Have I never exploited others for my own selfish gains? Have
I spoken out for equal treatment of all peoples, regardless of
color, creed, gender, sexual orientation, age, class?

The rancorous debate subsided and the meeting ended quietly. No resolution was reached that night. Thanksgiving vaca-
tion soon followed, and all the students left the campus. But
exactly one year later a Jewish faculty colleague told me that my
urging for self-reflection had hit home for many people, defusing
the tension and opening the possibility for real dialogue.

The self-questioning that I had proposed came from the
experience of visiting the remains of Dachau concentration camp
one summer several years ago. The real impact of the Holocaust
did not really hit me until that unplanned visit. The first stop of
a three-week European sightseeing tour that my wife and I made
was Munich, Germany. My primary reason for visiting Dachau,
located near Munich, was a news article that I happened to read.
It reported a reunion held in San Francisco between Dachau
camp survivors and Japanese-American soldiers of the U.S.
442nd Regimental Combat Team. These soldiers were the first
to liberate one of the subcamps of Dachau on April 14, 1944,
but the news had been suppressed by the U.S. government for

almost half a century, because the families of many of these American soldiers of Japanese descent were still incarcerated behind barbed-wire fences in the U.S.

Upon seeing the photographs of atrocities committed against the Jewish people, the purpose of my trip changed dramatically from sightseeing to a historical tracing of Jewish persecution wherever we went: Salzburg, Vienna, Budapest, Warsaw, Gdansk, Cracow, Auschwitz, Prague, and Amsterdam. At every stop I asked myself: If I had been a young man during World War II in these places, would I have been the victim or the victimizer?

In contemporary history Hitler is regarded as evil incarnate, and Mother Teresa as the embodiment of love. Their glaring difference is unequivocal, but both are human beings. Being human, we can be either a Hitler or a Mother Teresa. The key question for each of us becomes, Which am I, a Hitler or a Mother Teresa?

When Mother Teresa was once asked why she dedicated her life to the poor and needy of Calcutta, she is said to have replied, "Because I realized that I had a Hitler within me." This may sound paradoxical, but her admission penetrates to the core of religious awakening. Without awareness of one's own potential for evil, the demonic within remains unrecognized and unchecked. The potential to wreak havoc, whether in personal life or in society, awaits to explode from within us at any time. But once we become fully aware of our darkness, evil will lose its power over us, and the energy that propels it may be transformed into a power for good.

THE SINGLE
THREAD

42

南
無
阿
彌
陀
佛

In the middle of his life, after being confused as
to his true vocation and envious of his friends
successful in their careers, Basho declared his singular devotion to haiku poetry. At one time he
had thoughts of becoming a high government official and at another time achieving ecclesiastical
prominence. But he abandoned them all and
committed himself to the art of haiku poetry,
declaring: "Lacking ability and talent in everything else, I connect myself to this one thread
alone." This thread for Basho united life, nature,
and the universe into a single whole.

In fact, Basho claims that a common thread
weaves together the finest achievements of Japanese culture—Saigyo in traditional poetry, Sogi
in linked verse, Sesshu in sumi painting, Rikyu in
the art of tea ceremony, and his own craft of
haiku. This singular thread endures even today,

uniting aesthetic creativity (human) and cosmic creativity (nature).

Confucius was a great thinker, who lived in the Axial Age of world history. According to Karl Jaspers, who coined this term, his contemporaries include Lao-tzu and Mo-tzu in China, Buddha and Mahavira in India, Socrates and Plato in Greece, and the prophets of Israel—Isaiah, Jeremiah, and the Second Isaiah. His students revered him as an erudite teacher of incomparable wisdom, but Confucius rejected such accolades, saying, "I have only one thread upon which I string them all." That single thread was conscientiousness (*chung*) to oneself and to others, the basis of ethical life. That golden thread wove together one of the grandest tapestries of world civilization, influencing the course of the entire East Asian world.

While both Basho and Confucius were geniuses and discovered their respective callings, Saichi was but a simple, unlettered woodworker, who was called to a life of singular commitment:

> Having received the single thread of nembutsu
> Unmistakable is the one path that I take;
> Walking together with namu-amida-butsu
> As deep as Saichi's heart—
> Nay, even deeper is Amida's heart.

For Saichi the single thread of nembutsu had already been chosen for him by the Primal Vow of Amida. Coming from the heart of great compassion, infinitely deeper than anything humanly conceivable, the single thread of nembutsu is a gift given freely to anyone who seeks a unifying center in life. Nembutsu practice is utterly simple, but at the same time incomparably effective in leading to liberation and freedom, because it is the working of the Buddha that helps us negotiate through the blind passions of greed and anger.

Toward the end of his long and productive life of ninety years, Shinran in Kyoto receives his former disciples from far-away Kanto district. Traveling more than four hundred miles by foot, they call on their teacher seeking clarification on the finer points of doctrine. But Shinran declines to answer, urging them instead to go seek the learned monks of the monasteries in Nara and Mt. Hiei for answers to doctrinal questions. His own reply is clear and unequivocal:

> As for myself, Shinran, I simply receive the words of my dear teacher Honen, "Just say the nembutsu and be saved by Amida," and entrust myself to the Primal Vow. Besides this there is nothing else. (*Tannisho* II)

How disappointed his followers must have been! Shinran, however, simply affirms the only thing that truly matters in his life: the single thread of nembutsu that unifies the infinite past and the infinite future, the Primal Vow and the Pure Land, both here and now.

Knowledge of doctrine may be interesting but ultimately unnecessary, meditative practice may be meaningful but eventually unproductive, and moral virtue is to be applauded but fails to liberate us from delusion. Shinran concludes their meeting with the parting words: "In essence, such is the true entrusting practiced by this foolish one. Now, whether you accept the nembutsu and entrust yourself to it, or reject it, that is your decision."

In the single thread of nembutsu is contained ten kalpas of galactic time, all the compassion of countless universes, the sacrifices of innumerable bodhisattvas, the Buddha of Immeasurable

Light and Immeasurable Life, the Pure Land of peaceful rest.
They all come alive in each saying of namu-amida-butsu.

    Having turned away from the little paths
    Of myriad practices and good acts,
    I return to the Primal Vow, the one true reality,
    Quickly attaining the enlightenment that is nirvana.

EPILOGUE

Today, as I continue to walk on the white path through the river of fire and the river of water, the three questions that prompted my journey still remain as the basic framework of my life and worldview. In recent years that path has been greatly broadened and expanded, for the Primal Vow itself is the great white path. And the Primal Vow as the working of great compassion provides ample room for the bandits of sundry teachings and the beasts of blind passions to co-exist with me on the path. Unlike the parable in which the traveler alone walks the path, leaving behind the bandits and beasts on the eastern shore, they all walk beside me, reminding me of my reality as a limited karmic being subject to all kinds of temptations. But altogether we shall attain complete liberation and freedom that is the Pure Land on the farther shore.

Just as the bandits and beasts will always be with me as long as I remain a karma-bound being, so too the river of fire and the river of water will remain inseparable from the white path. Although the rivers have subsided and appear calm, I know that they can turn into searing flames and lashing waves in an instant.

That is, my greed, symbolized by water, is insatiable, because I want to live forever and negotiate life according to my self-centered calculations. And my anger, symbolized by fire, remains under control, but the moment things do not turn out according to my wish, it may explode. Even though others cannot see the greed and the anger hidden within me, they are as real as the river of fire and the river of water that make up the parable.

Since my karmic life is unthinkable without the bandits and beasts, the fire and water, I cannot but follow the injunction of Sakyamuni Buddha and hear the call of Amida Buddha. Even when my focus gets blurred and my interest wanes, the saying of nembutsu brings me back to the reality of the white path.

As a closure, I return to the three questions with which my journey began in the order of their significance. First, who am I? Whence do I come? Wither do I go? The answer is simple. I am a limited karmic being, full of ignorance and forever wandering, who has been endowed with a gift, the single thread of nembutsu. Guided by the single thread of nembutsu, I emerge from the darkness of countless past lives and see the light of day that enables me to become truly and really myself. I have arrived, I have come home. The agitations and chaos in my life are part of my reality, knowing full well that my ultimate destiny is the Pure Land of Immeasurable Light and Life.

Second, what is the one word of compassion? I realize now that it's not so much the word but the source that is crucial. No matter how articulate a person may be, if the word comes from a limited intellect and calculating mind, it will be mere word play (*prapanca*), covering up one's ignorance and never reaching the depth of human feeling. But this awareness enables me to give up discursive strategies as an answer and to entrust myself to the reality of great compassion. From its depth, then, emerges the genuine word (*desana*) that uplifts all of life as is. It may appear as a single word, or an eloquent silence, or namu-amida-butsu itself.

Finally, is my friend who took his own life happy now? Who is to say? As far as I am concerned, I have no choice but to entrust myself to the working of great compassion that vowed to work ceaselessly until all beings, even a single blade of grass, are liberated into the universe of boundless light. I need no convincing that my friend now lives in the heart of great compassion, beyond any measure of happiness or unhappiness. He joins the chorus of countless enlightened beings in the universe all praising the Name of Amida, and whenever I hear namu-amida-butsu being intoned, I hear his reassuring voice that all is well.

> The eye that sees what cannot be seen,
> The ear that hears what cannot be heard,
> The body that knows what is not known.
>
> —Kanjiro Kawai

ENDNOTES

The references mentioned in the endnotes are meant for readers who wish to explore the world of Shin Buddhism, especially the religious thought of Shinran. Mostly those sources available in English are given, although a few sources in Japanese are listed for those interested. In order to maintain the flow of the narrative I have frequently modified the existing translations, or given my own rendition of Shinran's works.

One of the best readable introductions to Shinran's thought is Hee-Sung Keel's *Understanding Shinran* (Fremont, CA: Asian Humanities Press, 1995). Written by a Christian scholar of comparative religion at Sogang University in Korea, the book is sympathetic but critical and will inspire readers to learn more about Shin Buddhism.

For a general description of the life and thought of Shinran, Alfred Bloom's pioneering effort, *Shinran's Gospel of Pure Grace* (Phoenix: University of Arizona, 1965), still remains a standard work. It has undergone several reprintings and is frequently used as a college textbook.

The work by Yoshifumi Ueda and Dennis Hirota, *Shinran: An Introduction to His Thought* (Kyoto: Hongwanji International Center, 1989), is recommended for advanced students. The value of this work lies in the abundant citations of Shinran's own writings on central topics in Shin Buddhism.

The only available general survey of Pure Land Buddhism is *The Pure Land Tradition: History and Development*, edited by James Foard, Michael Solomon, and Richard Payne (Berkeley Buddhist Studies Number 3, 1996). Although the volume is not meant to be a comprehensive history and the chapters by twelve different scholars lack coherence, no other comparable work exists. It includes two chapters on India, four on China, and six on Japan.

A valuable contribution to Pure Land studies is found in a recent work by Luis O. Gomez, *The Land of Bliss: The Paradise of the Buddha of Measureless Light* (Honolulu: University of Hawai'i Press, 1996, and Kyoto: Shinshu Otani-ha, 1996). The work contains translations of both the Sanskrit and Chinese versions of the *Larger Sutra of Pure Land* or the *Larger Sukhavativyuha Sutra* and the *Smaller Sutra of Pure Land* or the *Smaller Sukhavativyuha Sutra.* Especially helpful is Appendix 3, For Further Study, which contains a complete bibliography on the basic Pure Land scriptures and secondary sources.

These two sutras, as well as the *Sutra on the Contemplating Amida Buddha,* have also been translated by Hisao Inagaki in *The Three Pure Land Sutras,* published in the English Tripitaka series by Bukkyo Dendo Kyokai, also known as BDK (Berkeley: Numata Center for Buddhist Research and Publication, 1995). Since this work contains the Triple Sutra in a single volume, I have made reference to this work together with the Gomez translation.

For those interested in my own interpretation of Shinran, I suggest the following: "Shinran: The New Path to Buddhahood" in *The Pure Land Tradition: History and Development,* noted above; "The Nature of Religious Experience in Shin Buddhism," *The Other Side of God,* ed. Peter Berger (New York: Anchor Books, 1981); "Interior Practice in Shin Buddhism," *The Pacific World,* n.s., No. 1 (Fall 1990); and "When Broken Tiles Become Gold," *Of Human Bondage and Divine Grace,* ed. John Ross Carter (La Salle, IL: Open Court, 1992).

The major works of Shinran in English translations noted below may be obtained by writing to the following addresses:

Buddhist Study Center Press
1727 Pali Highway
Honolulu, Hawaii 96813
(808) 973-6135

Buddhist Bookstore
1710 Octavia Street
San Francisco, CA 94109
(415) 776-7877

SHIN BUDDHISM TRANSLATION SERIES (abbreviated SBTS)

Complete translation of Shinran's works, published by the Hongwanji International Center, Kyoto. The General Editor for this series is Yoshifumi Ueda, and the Head of the translation committee is Dennis Hirota.

The True Teaching, Practice and Realization of the Pure Land Way, translation of Shinran's major work, *Kyogyoshinsho*, in four volumes: Vol. I (1983), Vol. II (1985), Vol. III (1987), and Vol. IV (1990). D. T. Suzuki also translated the first four of this six-chapter work as one of the final projects of his life. It was published posthumously as *The Kyogyoshinsho: The Collection of Passages Expounding the True Teaching, Living, Faith and Realizing of the Pure Land* (Kyoto: Otaniha Shumusho, 1969).

Letters of Shinran, translation of *Mattosho* (1978)
Notes on 'Essentials of Faith Alone,' translation of *Yuishinsho-mon'i* (1979)
Notes on Once-calling and Many-calling, translation of *Ichinen-tanen mon'i* (1980)
Notes on Inscriptions on Sacred Scrolls, translation of *Songo-shinzo meimon* (1981)
Passages on the Pure Land Way, translation of *Jodo-monrui jusho* (1983)
Hymns of the Pure Land, translation of *Jodo-wasan* (1991)
Hymns of the Pure Land Masters, translation of *Oso wasan* (1992)
Hymns of the Dharma-Ages, translation of *Shozomatsu-wasan* (1993)
All of the above, plus other works by Shinran, were recently published together as *The Collected Works of Shinran*, Vol. I Writings and Vol. II Introductions, Glossaries, and Reading Aids (Kyoto: Jodoshinshu Nishi Hongwanji, 1997).

RYUKOKU TRANSLATION SERIES
(abbreviated RTS)

Published by Ryukoku University, Kyoto, the main institution of higher learning of the Honpa (Nishi) Hongwanji Branch of Shin Buddhism. These works contain both the original Japanese text and English translation, produced by a translation committee under the editorship of different faculty members at Ryukoku University.

The Shoshinge, Gatha of True Faith in the Nembutsu (1961)
Tannisho, Notes Lamenting Differences (1962)
The Jodo Wasan, The Hymns on the Pure Land (1965)
The Kyo Gyo Shin Sho, The Teaching, Practice, Faith, and Enlightenment (1966). Selected passages only.
The Koso Wasan, The Hymns on the Patriarchs (1974)
Shozomatsu Wasan, The Hymns on the Last Age (1980)

TEXTS FREQUENTLY CITED

The following abbreviations are used for texts frequently cited in the endnotes.

Buddhist Voices   *Buddhist Voices from Metta* (Honolulu: Buddhist Study Center Press, 1996). Contains selected articles carried in the *Metta*, the official newsletter of the Buddhist Study Center, over a twenty-five-year period. The BSC Press, under the general editorship of Ruth Tabrah, has also published many works on Shin Buddhism, one of the most recent being *Dharma Treasures: Spiritual Insights from Hawaii's Shin Buddhist Pioneers* (1997) by Tatsuo Muneto, which is cited in the endnotes as simply *Dharma Treasures*.

Land of Bliss   *The Land of Bliss* by Luis Gomez mentioned above. The page numbers given refer to the translation from the Chinese Pure Land sutras, since they form the basis of Shin Buddhism.

Pure Land Sutras   *The Three Pure Land Sutras*, tr. Hisao Inagaki, includes *The Sutra on the Contemplation of Amitayus*, which is not contained in *The Land of Bliss*.

Pure Land Tradition   *The Pure Land Tradition: History and Development*, as noted above.

MCB   *Mysticism: Christian and Buddhist* by D. T. Suzuki (New York: Harper and Brothers, 1957). This work contains the largest number of Saichi poems translated into English. According to one count, Saichi left more than ten thousand religious poems written down on thirty notebooks.

Shukyo shijin   *Shukyo shijin Saichi* (The Religious Poet Saichi) by Fuji Shusui (Kyoto: Chojiya, 1963). The author who was a poet himself gives a sensitive interpretation of Saichi's poems.

Tannisho   *Tannisho: A Shin Buddhist Classic* (Honolulu: Buddhist Study Center Press, 2nd Revised Edition, 1996). This is the author's translation with an explanatory Afterword. Compiled about thirty years after Shinran's death by Yui-en, it contains the sayings of Shinran and doctrinal disputes that occured at that time. For complete bibliography, see Alfred Bloom, *Strategies for Modern Living: A Commentary with Text of the Tannisho* (Berkeley: Numata Center for Buddhist Research and Publication, 1992), pp. 179–81.

True Teaching   *The True Teaching, Practice and Realization of the Pure Land Way*, the major opus by Shinran, published in four volumes in the SBTS as noted above.

PROLOGUE

p. xxii. The parable of the two rivers and white path appears in Shinran, *True Teaching*, II, pp. 220–24.

This parable is one of the major genres of Pure Land art; for examples, see John Rosenfield and Elizabeth ten Grotenhuis, *Journey of the Three Jewels* (New York: Asian Society, 1979), pp. 133–37; and Joji Okazaki, *Pure Land Buddhist Paintings* (Tokyo: Kodansha International, 1977), pp. 147–50. Scroll paintings of this parable are found in the Cleveland Art Museum and the Seattle Art Museum.

The parable forms the theme of some Japanese gardens. Among those that I have seen are the gardens of Komyoji in Kyoto, the headquarters of the Seizan Jodo School; Zenkoji in Takayama city; Inkuji in the outskirts of Kyoto; and Taima-dera. For the latter, see the article by Elizabeth ten Grotenhuis, "The White Path Crossing Two Rivers: a contemporary Japanese garden represents the past," *Journal of Garden History*, Vol. 15, No. 1 (January-March 1995), 1–17.

For an informative Jungian analysis of this parable, see J. Marvin Spiegelman and Mokusen Miyuki, *Buddhism and Jungian Psychology* (Phoenix: Falcon Press, 1985), pp. 137–47.

p. xxv. Quotation from Leo Tolstoy, *The Death of Ivan Ilyich* (New York: Bantam Books, 1981), p. 126.

1. THE HISTORICAL LEGACY

p. 1. For study of early Pure Land scriptures and doctrines, see Fujita, "Pure Land Buddhism in India," *Pure Land Tradition*, pp. 1–31.

p. 5. Shinran's poem, *The Hymns on the Patriarchs* No. 94, p. 119. The number refers to the verse in the original Japanese edition, *Shinshu shogyo zensho* (Kyoto: Kokyo shoin, 1957), followed by the page number.

2. THE COLOR GOLD

p. 7. The third vow, see *Land of Bliss*, p. 166, and *Pure Land Sutras*, p. 32.

p. 7. Dharma as "teaching" *(desana)* and as "reality-as-is" *(adhigama-dharma)* is discussed in Jikido Takasaki, *A Study of the Ratnagotravibhaga* (Roma: Istituto Italianao per il Medeo ed Estremo Oriente, 1966), p. 182.

p. 8. This verse is from *Land of Bliss*, p. 146, and *Pure Land Sutras*, p. 122.

p. 8. The bits of rubble metaphor appears in *Notes on 'Essentials of Faith Alone,'* p. 41. "When we entrust ourselves to the Tathagata's Primal Vow, we, who are like bits of tile and pebbles, are turned into gold. Peddlers and hunters, who are like stones and tiles and pebbles, are grasped and never abandoned by the Tathagata's light."

3. THE SPIRIT OF THE VALLEY

pp. 10–11. This translation is from Arthur Waley, *The Way and Its Power: A Study of the Tao Te Ching and Its Place in Chinese Thought* (New York: Grove Press, 1958), p. 149.

p. 12. Hillman quoted in *Care of the Soul* by Thomas Moore (New York: HarperCollins, 1992), p. 9.

4. HOME COMPOSTING

pp. 14–15. Poem from *Buddhist Voices*, p. 88.

pp. 16–17. Tz'u-min quoted by Shinran in *Notes on 'Essentials of Faith Alone,'* p. 36, and in *True Teaching* III, pp. 117–18.

p. 17. Quotation from Ichitaro in Tetsuo Unno, *Jodoshinshu Buddhism* (San Francisco: Heian International, 1980), p. 109.

p. 17. *A Healing Path: A Soul Approach to Illness* (New York: Arkana, 1995), p. 70.

p. 17. For Bernardin quotation, see "Death as a Friend," *The New York Times Magazine*, December 1, 1996.

5. PRIMAL VOW

p. 19. Metaphors for Primal Vow as magnet and earth, *True Teaching* I, p. 157.

p. 20. The Japanese Garden for Reflection and Contemplation at Smith College was designed by David Slawson, author of *Secret Teachings in the Art of Japanese Garden* (Tokyo: Kodansha International, 1987).

p. 22. *Tannisho*, p. 33.

pp. 22–23. The eighteenth vow of Amida Buddha according to Shinran's reading is found in *Shinran: An Introduction to His Thought*, pp. 185–94. For the original Chinese, *Land of Bliss*, p. 167, and *Pure Land Sutras*, p. 34.

p. 23. Fulfillment of the eighteenth vow, according to Shinran, see *Shinran: An Introduction to His Thought*, pp. 195–202. For the original Chinese version, *Land of Bliss*, p. 187, and *Pure Land Sutras*, p. 54.

p. 24. Shinran on exclusion clause, *Letters of Shinran*, pp. 58–59.

p. 25. *Tannisho*, p. 33.

6. NEMBUTSU:
THE NAME-THAT-CALLS

p. 27. For the relationship between *amitabha* and *amitayus*, see Fujita, *Pure Land Tradition*, pp. 11–16.

p. 29. *Way of the Pilgrim*, trans. R. M. French (New York: HarperCollins, 1991), pp. 14 and 87, respectively.

p. 29. *On the Invocation of the Name of Jesus* by A Monk of the Eastern Church (London: Fellowship of St. Alban and St. Sergius, no date).

p. 30. The Chinese for namu-amida-butsu is *namo o-mi-t'o-fo*, and the Sanskrit is *namo 'mitabhaya buddhaya*.

p. 33. *Tannisho*, p. 11.

p. 34. Poem by Jutaro Oshima, *Dharma Treasures*, p. 35.

pp. 34–35. Ogui episode related in the Cleveland Buddhist Temple Newsletter (April 28, 1996). A collection of Ogui's articles will appear as *Zen Shin Talks*, edited by Mary K. Gove and published by Zen Shin Buddhist publication, Cleveland.

7. OTHER POWER

p. 36. For the story of Dharmakara Bodhisattva, see *Land of Bliss*, pp. 161–76, and *Pure Land Sutras*, pp. 27–45. The story is not a story but of reality emerging into human consciousness.

p. 37. Saichi's poem in D. T. Suzuki, *Myokonin Asahara Saichi shū* [Collected Sayings of Saichi] (Tokyo: Shunjūsha, 1967), p. 174, No. 67. This contains the most comprehensive collection of Saichi's poems in print.

p. 38. Epstein, *Thoughts Without a Thinker* (New York: Basic Books, 1995), p. 113.

p. 38. Ignatow, *Against the Evidence* (Hanover and London: Wesleyan University Press, 1993), p. 124. I am indebted to Abram Yoshida for calling my attention to this collection of poetry.

p. 39. Two poems by Haru Matsuda in *Dharma Treasures*, pp. 8–9.

p. 41. *Tannisho*, p. 10.

8. SELF-POWER

p. 42. For Shinran's definition of self-power, see *Notes on 'Essentials of Faith Alone,'* p. 40.

p. 43. Jung, *Psychology and Religion* (New Haven: Yale University Press, 1938), p. 102.

pp. 44–45. Kichibei's quote from Kusunoki Kyō, ed., *Myokonin Monodane Kichibei Goroku* [Sayings of Myokonin Kichibei] (Kyoto: Hōzōkan, 1991), p. 303.

9. THE QUEST

p. 48. T. S. Eliot, *The Complete Poems and Plays 1909–1950* (New York: Harcourt, Brace & Co., 1952), "The Dry Salvages," p. 136.

p. 50. Hamada quotation from Yanagi Soetsu, *The Unknown Craftsman* (Tokyo: Kodansha International, 1972), p. 224.

p. 51. Uchiyama quotation from his *Opening the Hand of Thought: Approach to Zen* (New York: Penguin Books, 1993), p. 61.

p. 51. Dogen on "Birth and Death," trans. Masao Abe and Norman Waddell, *The Eastern Buddhist*, n.s., Vol. V, No. 1 (May 1972), pp. 78–80.

10. UNHINDERED LIGHT

p. 54. "This Tathagata is light" is found in *Notes on Once-calling and Many-calling*, p. 46.

p. 54. "The light dispels the darkness" in *Hymns of the Pure Land* (No. 1), p. 13.

p. 54. Bloom, *Shinran's Gospel of Pure Grace*, p. 57.

p. 54. *Smaller Sutra* in *Land of Bliss*, p. 147, and *Pure Land Sutras*, p. 122.

p. 55. *Contemplation Sutra* in *Pure Land Sutras*, p. 105.

p. 55. Verse on 84,000 delusions, *Shukyo shijin*, p. 145.

p. 56. Ikeyama poem, *Shin o yuku tabibito* [Traveler on the path of true entrusting] (Kyoto: Ichidoe, 1971), pp. 220–21.

pp. 56–57. Shinran poem, *Hymns of the Pure Land Masters* (No. 39), p. 31.

p. 57. Shinran quotation, *True Teaching* I, pp. 137–38.

11. FAITH AS TRUE ENTRUSTING

p. 59. Tillich, *Courage to Be* (New Haven: Yale University Press, 1952), p. 190.

p. 62. Shinran quotation, *True Teaching* II, p. 204.

p. 62. Poem from *Shukyo shijin*, p. 272.

12. AWAKENING

p. 63. Martin Heidegger, *Discourse on Thinking* (New York: Harper and Row, 1966), p. 24. Meditative thinking is further explored in Heidegger's *What Is Called Thinking?* (New York: Harper and Row, 1968). Contained within it is the calling, reminiscent of the function of the Name-that-calls: "Thinking, then, is here not taken as an occurrence whose course is open to psychological observation. Nor is thinking conceived merely as an activity that obeys norms and a scale of values. Thinking can be guided only if it has in itself a calling, directing it to what there is to-be-thought. The question, 'What is This that calls on us to think?,' if asked with sufficient urgency, brings us also to the problem *that* thinking, *qua* thinking, is essentially a call," pp. 160–61.

p. 65. Quotation from Barasch, *The Healing Path*, p. 372.

p. 65. For Hakuin, see Isshu Miura and Ruth Fuller Sasaki, *The Zen Koan* (New York: Harcourt Brace and Weld, 1965), p. 26.

13. TRANSFORMATION

p. 67. The Seventeen-Article Constitution in *Sources of the Japanese Tradition*, eds. Ryusaku Tsunoda, *et al.* (New York: Columbia University Press, 1964), Vol. I, pp. 47–51.

p. 68. The two poems are by K. Takebe, quoted in Yonezawa Hideo, *Shin to wa nanika* (What is true entrusting?), pp. 219 and 221

p. 69. *Julian of Norwich: Showings*, trans. Edmund Colledge and James Walsh (New York: Paulist Press, 1978), p. 258.

p. 70. For definition of virtue, see Tillich, who interprets the Greek *arete* in *Courage to Be*, p. 83. See also Nishitani's definition of *virtus* as the "individual capacity that each being possesses as a display of its own possibility of existence," *Religion and Nothingness* (Berkeley: University of California Press, 1984), p. 123.

p. 70. The transformation of karmic evil, *Notes on 'Essentials of Faith Alone,'* p. 32.

pp. 71–72. These two famous verses on ice and water are found in *Hymns of the Pure Land Masters* (Nos. 39 and 40), p. 31.

14. TWO KINDS OF COMPASSION

p. 73. All quotations on compassion in this section are from *Tannisho*, p. 7.

p. 75. Kichibei's story in Yanagi, *The Unknown Craftsman*, p. 155.

p. 76. Shinran, *Hymns of the Dharma Ages* (Nos. 95 and 96), p. 67.

15. CONSPIRACY OF GOOD

p. 80. Dalai Lama, *Tibetan Portrait: The Power of Compassion* (New York: Rizzoli International Publications, 1996). No page numbers.

p. 81. Story of girl in coma is from *Jodoshinshu Buddhism*, p. 50.

p. 83. Shinran poem, *Hymns of the Pure Land Masters* (No. 95), p. 73.

p. 84. A month-long celebration in honor of Sugihara was held in New York City according to *The New York Times*, November 8, 1995. For his life, see Hillel Levine, *In Search of Sugihara* (New York: Free Press, 1996), a fascinating account of research on Sugihara's life, interviewing Jewish survivors in Europe, America, Australia, and Japan. A personal recollection by the wife is found in Yukiko Sugihara, *Visas for Life* (San Francisco: Edwards Brothers, 1995).

16. ATTAINMENT WITHOUT A TEACHER

p. 87. Accounts of this school are from a private journal, *Jikō* (Light of Compassion), Vol. 28, No. 6, p. 20.

p. 88. Simone Weil, *Waiting for God* (New York: G. P. Putnam's Sons, 1951), p. 114.

17. HUMILITY

p. 91. On bowing, see Shunryu Suzuki, *Zen Mind, Beginner's Mind* (New York: Weatherhill, 1970), pp. 43–44.

p. 91. *Scripture of the Lotus Blossom of the Fine Dharma*, trans. Leon Hurvitz (New York: Columbia University Press, 1976), pp. 279–85.

p. 91. Ichitaro quotation, *Jodoshinshu Buddhism*, p. 112.

p. 92. Lindo Poem, *Buddhist Voices*, p. 43.

p. 93. For an alternate translation from Confucius, see Arthur Waley, *The Analects of Confucius* (New York: Random House, 1938), p. 188.

18. ARROGANCE

pp. 98–99. Dialogue on hypocrisy, Soetsu Yanagai, *Inaba no Genza* (Kyoto: Otani Shuppan, 1950), pp. 21–22.

19. TRUE DISCIPLE OF BUDDHA

p. 100. Tillich, "You Are Accepted," *The Shaking of the Foundation* (New York: Charles Scribner's Sons, 1948), pp. 153–63.

p. 100. On the True Disciple of Buddha, *True Teaching* II, pp. 265–79.

p. 102. Shinran's confession, *True Teaching* II, p. 279.

p. 103. Shinran's words of joy, *True Teaching* I, pp. 140–41.

20. MYOKONIN

p. 104. The myokonin became popular in Japan after D. T. Suzuki delved into their life stories that were compiled in the nineteenth century. Sources on the myokonin in English are extremely limited. For a concise discussion, see the forthcoming *Buddha of Infinite Light* (Boston: Shambhala Press, 1998), which is a revised second edition of Suzuki's *Shin Buddhism* (New York: Harper and Row, 1970).

The following works by Suzuki also contain sections on the subject: *Mysticism: Christian and Buddhist* (New York: Harper and Brothers, 1957); *Japanese Spirituality* (Japan Society for the Promotion of Science, 1972); and *Collected Writings on Shin Buddhism* (Kyoto: Shinshu Otaniha, 1973).

See also Zenshō Asaeda, ed., *Various Problems of Myōkōnin-den* (Kyoto: Nagata Bunshodo, 1987). Articles in English by Alfred Bloom, Hisao Inagaki, Leslie Kawamura, and Yanagi Soetsu, pp. 429–500. Kawamura gives a brief historical background on the compilation of Myokonin stories, pp. 40–55.

pp. 106–7. Two poems from *MCB*, pp. 202 and 213, respectively.

21. LOTUS BLOOMS IN FIRE

p. 108. The phrase "lotus blooms in fire" is found in the Chinese translation of the *Vimalakirti-nirdesa Sutra* but not in the Tibetan version. Compare the English translation from Kumarjiva, *The Vimalakiriti Nirdesa Sutra* by Charles Luk, 90, "lotus blossoming in scorching fire," and the corresponding passage in the translation from the Tibetan by Robert Thurman, *The Holy Teaching of Vimalakirti*, p. 70, "Just as it can be shown that a lotus / Cannot exist in the center of fire, / So they show the ultimate unreality / Of both pleasures and trances." Some scholars believe that the Chinese translation is closer to the lost Sanskrit original.

The symbolism of lotus and fire occurs in Hinduism, see T. Goudriaan, *Kasyapa's Book of Wisdom* (1965) on "lotus fire," pp. 30–39. I am grateful to Dennis Hudson for this reference.

22. OCEAN OF THE PRIMAL VOW

p. 113. Verse from *Hymns of the Pure Land Masters* (No. 41), p. 31.

p. 114. Ibid., (No. 42), p. 32.

23. ONE BRIGHT PEARL

p. 115. Saichi, *MCB*, p. 191.

pp. 115–16. "One Bright Pearl," trans. Masao Abe and Norman Waddell, *The Eastern Buddhist*, n.s., Vol. IV, No. 2, pp. 108–17.

24. THE CRY OF CICADAS

p. 118. An alternate translation of this poem is found in *The Narrow Road to the Deep North and Other Travel Sketches*, trans. Nobuyuki Yuasa (New York: Penguin Books, 1966), p. 123: "In the utter silence / Of a temple / A cicada's voice alone / Penetrates the rocks."

25. AS IS: *SONO-MAMA*

p. 122. "Self-so" and "always so" by Waley, *The Way and Its Power*, pp. 174 and 209. See also the rendition *tzu-jan* as, "It was always and of itself so," p. 205.

p. 123. Ichitaro quotation, *Jodoshinshu Buddhism*, p. 113.

p. 124. Shinran's poem, *The Hymns on the Pure Land* (No. 70), p. 61.

26. DUALITY

p. 126. "Believing in the Mind," trans. D. T. Suzuki, *Manual of Zen Buddhism* (New York: Grove Press, 1960), p. 76.

pp. 129–30. Two quotations from Nietzsche, *The Will to Power*, trans. Walter Kaufmann and R. J. Hollingdale (New York: Vintage Books, 1967), pp. 298 (No. 552d) and 268 (No. 484).

p. 130. Martin Buber, *I and Thou*, trans. Ronald Gregor Smith (New York: Charles Scribner's Sons, 1957). This translation is preferred over the version by Walter Kaufman (New York: Charles Scribner's Sons, 1970).

p. 130. Duality in Tillich, first quotation from *Theology of Culture* (Oxford: University Press, 1959), pp. 4–5; second quotation from *Dynamics of Faith* (New York: Harper and Row, 1957), p. 12.

p. 130. Nonduality in Tillich, *Dynamics of Faith*, p. 11.

pp. 130–31. Suzuki, *Manual of Zen Buddhism*, p. 81.

27. NONDUALITY

p. 132. For introductory discussion, see David Loy, *Nonduality: A Study in Comparative Philosophy* (New Haven: Yale University Press, 1988).

p. 132. James, *Varieties of Religious Experience* (New York: Vintage Books, 1990), p. 192.

p. 133. Poem from *Su Tung-p'o*, trans. Burton Watson (New York: Columbia University Press, 1965), p. 107.

p. 133. Basho, *The Narrow Raod to the Deep North and Other Travel Sketches*, p. 33.

p. 133. Magic Johnson in Michael Murphy and Rhea A. White, *In the Zone: Transcendent Experience in Sports* (New York: Penguin Books, 1995), p. 125.

p. 134. John Brodie, *In the Zone*, p. 118. The problem pointed out by Brodie is evident in such works as *Sacred Hoop: Spiritual Lessons of a Hardwood Warrior* (New York: Hyperion, 1995) by Phil Jackson, coach of the world champion Chicago Bulls. The application of Zen to sports may be interesting but has nothing to do with Zen, which deals with the question of living and dying.

p. 136. Saichi in *Japanese Spirituality*, p. 189.

28. INTERDEPENDENCE

p. 137. Dalai Lama quoted in *Tibetan Portrait: The Power of Compassion*. No page numbers.

p. 138. Story about Genza in Haguri Gyodo, *Genza dogyo monogatari* [Tales of Genza] (Kyoto: Hyakkaen, 1950), p. 203.

pp. 139–40. *The Blooming of a Lotus* (Boston: Beacon Press, 1993), p. 124.

This work demonstrates the author's profound knowledge of Buddhist thought and its practical application for healing and transformation.

p. 141. Ichitaro quotation, *Jodoshinshu Buddhism*, p. 114.

p. 141. Aida poem quoted in the New York Buddhist Church Newsletter (July 1996).

pp. 141–42. *Tannisho*, p. 8.

29. SELF AS DYNAMIC FLOW

p. 143. For a discussion of ki, see Yuasa Yasuo, *The Body, Self-Cultivation and Ki-Energy* (Albany: SUNY Press, 1993); and Thomas P. Kasulis, "The Body—Japanese Style," *Self as Body in Asian Theory and Practice*, eds. T. P. Kasulis, R. T. Ames, and W. Dissanayake (New York: SUNY Press, 1993), pp. 299–319.

p. 144. William James on the self, *The Principles of Psychology* (Cambridge: Harvard University Press, 1981), Vol. I, p. 280.

pp. 145–46. Saichi poem, *MCB*, p. 204.

30. ALL IS A CIRCLE

p. 147. The title comes from a poem in Nancy Wood, *War Cry on a Prayer Feather* (New York: Doubleday, 1979), p. 105.

p. 148. For succinct relationship between the physical, psychological, and spiritual in Aikido, see the author's brief Foreword in Kisshomaru Ueshiba, *The Spirit of Aikido* (New York: Kodansha International, 1984).

pp. 148–49. Kubose, *Everyday Suchness* (Chicago: The Dharma House, 1967), pp. 93–94.

pp. 149–50. *Black Elk Speaks* (Lincoln: University of Nebraska Press, 1988), pp. 194–96.

p. 150. Jung on mandala, see his *Mandala Symbolism* from *The Collected Works of C. G. Jung*, Vol. 9, Part I (Princeton: University Press, 1959). See also Giuseppe Tucci, *Theory and Practice of the Mandala* (New York: Samual Weiser, 1977).

p. 151. Saigyo, *Mirror for the Moon*, trans. William LaFleur (New York: Grove Press, 1977), p. 43.

p. 151. *Religion and Nothingness*, p. 146.

p. 152. See G. R. Evans, *Alan of Lille: The Frontiers of Theology in the Later Twelfth Century* (Cambridge: University Press, 1983), p. 73. I am grateful to my colleague Carol Zaleski for this reference.

p. 152. *Black Elk Speaks*, p. 43.

pp. 152–53. Shinran poems, *Hymns of the Pure Land* (Nos. 3 and 5), pp. 7 and 9.

p. 153. Genshin, quoted in *True Teaching* I, p. 134. For further comments on *isshiji*, see *True Teaching* II, pp. 236–37.

31. KNOW THYSELF

p. 155. For further information on the work of this psychiatrist, K. Kishimoto, see his *Ningen kaifuku no michi* [Way of Recovery of the Human] (Tokyo: Yayoi Shobo, 1984).

p. 156. Gadamer, *Philosophical Hermeneutics* (Berkeley: University of California Press, 1977), p. 57.

32. HELL IS MY ONLY HOME

p. 158. *Tannisho*, p. 5.

p. 159. On the six realms and its impact on Japanese literature, see William Lafleur, *The Karma of Words* (Berkeley: University of California Press, 1986), Chapter 2.

pp. 160–61. *Tannisho*, p. 6.

p. 161. Shinran, *Hymns of the Dharma-Ages* (No. 4), p. 5.

p. 162. Scholem, *Major Trends in Jewish Mysticism* (New York: Schocken, 1961), p. 236.

33. THE WORLD OF DEW

p. 163. Poem from Miner, *An Introduction to Japanese Court Poetry* (Stanford: University Press, 1968), p. 91.

p. 164. Ryokan's first poem on Amida, Ryuichi Abe and Peter Haskell, *Great Fool: Zen Master Ryōkan* (Honolulu: University of Hawai'i Press, 1996), p. 207. For other poems related to Shin Buddhism, see Moriyama Ryuhei, *Ryokan: hyohaku no shi* [Ryokan: Poems of Wandering] (Tokyo: Yukonsha, 1975), pp. 136–39.

p. 165. Issa, *The Year of My Life*, trans. Nobuyuki Yuasa (Berkeley: University of California Press, 1972), p. 104.

34. UNREPEATABLE LIFE

p. 168. All the poems by Mrs. Takeuchi in this section are from a private printing and not available to the public.

pp. 171–72. Saichi, *MCB*, p. 195.

35. MY GRANDMOTHER

p. 175. Shan-tao quotation in *True Teaching* III, p. 492.

p. 177. First poem by Saichi, *MCB*, p. 16; second poem from Suzuki, *Myokonin Asahara Saichi shu* (Tokyo: Shunjusha, 1967), p. 387. This collection contains the greatest number of Saichi poems in one volume.

36. THE PURE LAND

p. 179. Shinran, *True Teaching* III, p. 395.

p. 179. On Pure Land, see Kotatsu Fujita, *Pure Land Tradition*, pp. 20–25. Also see his "The Origin of Pure Land," *The Eastern Buddhist*, n.s., Vol. XXIX, No. 1 (Spring 1996), pp. 38–51.

p. 181. Quotation regarding "immediately," *Notes on 'Essentials of Faith Alone,'* p. 35.

pp. 181–82. For brief discussion of ascent and descent, see Gadjin M. Nagao, *Mādhyamika and Yogācāra* (Albany: SUNY Press, 1991), pp. 201–7.

p. 182. *Hymns of the Pure Land* (No. 20), p. 21.

37. WHEN A PERSON DIES

p. 186. Dogen's total dynamic working, *Zenki*, trans. Masao Abe and Norman Waddell, *The Eastern Buddhist*, n.s., Vol. V, No. 1 (May 1972), pp. 74–77.

38. HOUSE OR HOME

p. 190. Both poems are from Saichi. See D. T. Suzuki, *Collected Writings on Shin Buddhism*, p. 88.

39. TRUE AND REAL LIFE

p. 191. This episode found in *Buddhist Voices*, pp. 103–5.

40. BUDDHA-NATURE

pp. 196–97. Shinran poem, *The Hymns of the Dharma-Ages* (No. 107), p. 73.

p. 197. Buddha-nature quotation, *Notes on 'Essentials of Faith Alone,'* p. 42.

pp. 197–98. Shinran poem, *Hymns of the Pure Land* (No. 94), p. 77.

p. 198. A brief summary of Tathagata-garbha thought is found in Paul Williams, *Mahayana Buddhism: The Doctrinal Foundations* (London: Routledge, 1989), pp. 96–115.

p. 198. Eliot develops his notion of mythosphere in *The Universal Myths* (New York: New American Library, 1976), *The Global Myths* (1993), and *The Timeless Myth* (1996), both published by Continuum, New York. The quotation is from *The Global Myths*, p. 33.

41. MOTHER TERESA AND HITLER

p. 201. For the liberation of Dachau, see personal recollection contained in Ellen Levine, *A Fence Away from Freedom* (New York: G. P. Putnam's Sons, 1992), pp. 126–29. For the most reliable and scholarly work on the Japanese-American internment during World War II, see Michi Weglyn, *Years of Infamy*, Second Revised Edition (Seattle: University of Washington Press, 1996). I would like to thank Michi for bringing my attention to the Levine book.

42. THE SINGLE THREAD

p. 203. Basho, *The Narrow Road to the Deep North*, p. 71. Yuasa translates the equivalent passage as follows: "The fact is, it knows no other art than the art of writing poetry, and therefore, it hangs on to it more or less blindly."

p. 204. For Axial Period, see Karl Jaspers, *The Origin and Goal of History* (London: Kegan Paul, 1953), pp. 1–21.

p. 204. For alternate translation of *chung*, see Wing-tsit Chan, *A Sourcebook in Chinese Philosophy*, p. 27: "*Chung* means the full development of one's [originally good mind] and *shu* means the extension of that mind to others."

p. 204. The single thread of nembutsu, *Shukyo shijin*, p. 95.

p. 205. *Tannisho*, p. 5.

p. 206. Shinran poem, *Hymns of the Pure Land Masters* (No. 53), p. 40.

p. 209. The saying by the renowned potter Kawai is from Yoshiko Uchida, *We Do Not Work Alone: The Thoughts of Kanjiro Kawai* (Kyoto: Nissha Printing Co., 1973), p. 8.

GLOSSARY OF KEY TERMS

Diacritical marks for foreign terms, omitted in the text, have been added.

Aikidō   Japanese martial art founded by Ueshiba Morihei (1883–1969), unifying various earlier forms of martial arts and advocating a nonviolent philosophy.

Amida   Amida is the East Asian combination of *amitābha* and *amitāyus*, Immeasurable Light and Immeasurable Life, respectively.

Amida Buddha   The Buddha of Immeasurable Life and Immeasurable Life, who as Dharmākara Bodhisattva fulfilled forty-eight vows to save all suffering beings and attained supreme enlightenment.

Avalokiteśvara   The bodhisattva of compassion, popularly known in East Asia as Kuan-yin (Chinese) or Kannon (Japanese). Amida's compassionate working is manifested in the form of Avalokiteśvara.

Bodhisattva   This term is used in two ways: any person who aspires for *bodhi* or enlightenment, and the bodily incarnation of enlightenment itself, such as Avalokiteśvara who manifests compassion. In early Buddhism it is also used to describe the previous lives of the historical Buddha.

Bonnō (klesha)   The original term literally means "that which agitates body and mind." This is translated as blind passion in our text.

Buddha-nature   The potential for enlightenment found in all beings and by extension the fundamental reality that permeates the phenomenal world.

Darkness of ignorance (*avidyā*).   The source of human suffering, personal and universal.

Deep hearing (*monpō*)   This practice, together with recitative nembutsu, constitutes Shin religious life.

Dharma   This term is derived from the Sanskrit root meaning maintain, support, or uphold; and in Buddhism it denotes each reality-as-it-is. When this reality is articulated, it becomes the teaching, hence, we speak of the Buddha Dharma.

Dharmākara Bodhisattva   The story of humanity's aspiration to resolve sufferings in the world, patterned after the life of the historical Buddha and culminating in the attainment of supreme enlightenment as Amida Buddha. It is more than a mere story for it is reality emerging in the life of one who seeks truth.

Dharmakāya   The fundamental reality that is beyond human conception and linguistic description. This is called *dharmatā dharmakāya* (dharmakāya-as-suchness) that appears in the human world of language as *upāya dharmakāya* (dharmakāya-as-compassion) and concretely manifested as namu-amida-butsu. Shinran explains the relationship between the two: "Dharmakāya-as-compassion arises out of dharmakaya-as-suchness, and dharmakāya-as-suchness arises or emerges into human consciousness as dharmakāya-as-compassion. These two aspects of dharmakāya differ but are not separate; they are one but not identical," *The Teaching* III, p. 376.

Dōjō   From the Sanskrit *bodhi-maṇḍa*, referring to the original place of Sakyamuni Buddha's enlightenment, and later used to refer to any training hall for religious practice. During Shinran's time, his followers gathered not at established temples but at ordinary dwellings called dōjō.

Duality   This characterizes our thinking whose function is to compare, discriminate, and analyze. The bifurcation involved is basically conceptual and discursive that has nothing to do with reality as it is.

Eighteenth Vow   This vow sums up the intent of all the forty-eight vows of Amida; hence it is called the Primal Vow.

Ensō   The circle drawn with a swift brush stroke, symbolizing emptiness as fullness, a favorite theme for calligraphy scrolls among Zen Buddhist masters.

Faith   Faith based on subject-object duality is summed up in the saying, "Assurance of things hoped for, the conviction of things not seen." This is to be differentiated from faith as true entrusting, based on nonduality, which is endowed by Amida Buddha to foolish beings.

Five great transgressions   Also translated as five grave offenses, it includes killing father, mother, and monk, spilling the blood of Buddha, and creating dissension in the religious community. In Mahayana Buddhism they include everything from criticism, censure, destruction of institutional Buddhism to disregard for the fundamental working of the karmic law.

Foolish being (*bonbu*)   A person who realizes human life as limited, imperfect, finite, and filled with the darkness of ignorance. In the words of Shinran, "As expressed in the parable of the two rivers and white path, we are full of ignorance and blind passion. Our desires are countless, and anger, wrath, jealousy, and envy are overwhelming, arising without pause; to the very last moment of life they do not cease, or disappear, or exhaust themselves." *Notes on Once-calling and Many-calling*, p. 48.

Forty-eight vows   The vows made by Dharmākara Bodhisattva on behalf of all suffering beings as described in the *Larger Sutra*.

Four Noble Truths   The basic teaching of the Buddha that 1) life does not move according to our wishes; hence, resulting in suffering, 2) the cause of suffering is insatiable greed, 3) the ideal state is free of greed and suffering, and 4) the way to liberation and freedom is the path taught by the Buddha.

Hakarai   This term means to plan, devise, calculate, and execute, and it is used in two ways. As a synonym of self-power, it refers to the dualistic thinking of foolish beings; and as descriptive of the working of Other Power, it denotes the design of the Primal Vow to save all beings.

Hell   The lowest of the six realms of existence, created by one's karmic ignorance.

Hua-yen   Major school of Chinese Buddhism, known in Japanese as
   Kegon.

Immeasurable Life   Quality of Amida as vowed in the thirteenth vow.

Immeasurable Light   Quality of Amida as vowed in the twelfth vow.

Interdependence   The central worldview of Mahayana Buddhism,
   based on dependent co-origination (*pratītya-samutpāda*).

Jesus Prayer   The saying of "Lord Jesus Christ have mercy upon me" or
   "upon me as a sinner," practiced in the Eastern Orthodox Church
   and developed into contemplative prayer in Hesychasm.

Jinen   The power of each being (*ji*) realizing itself, becoming what it
   was meant to become (*nen*).

Just sitting (*shikan-taza*)   The meditative practice of Soto Zen advocated
   by Dogen.

Kalpa   An infinitely long unit of time, metaphorically expressed, to
   connote the vast connections with the deep past.

Kalyanamitra   Literally, a good friend but is applied to a spiritual guide
   who teaches one to progress on the path of enlightenment.

Karma   From the Sanskrit root meaning "action," it led to the moral
   law of cause and effect. In Shin Buddhism, however, it is used to
   denote the limited, imperfect finite existence, referred to as karmic
   being, karma-bound being, or being of karmic evil.

Karmic evil   Here karma refers to the deep, unknown source of our
   darkness of ignorance that creates all kinds of negative consequences
   that cause suffering for oneself and others. Hence, it is called evil.

Ki   This term has two meanings. First, as a synonym of *chi'i* in Chinese,
   it connotes the vital energy that infuses the phenomenal world, including human beings. Second, as used in Shin Buddhist teaching of
   ki-hō ittai, it refers to the spiritual potential of a person (*ki*) that
   realizes itself in union (*ittai*) with the dharma or Amida Buddha (*hō*).

Kōan   The riddles that Rinzai Zen gives out to students who grapple
   with them for solutions. The most well-known koan is the question,
   "What is the sound of the one-hand clap?" popularized in J. D.
   Salinger's *Franny and Zooey*.

Listening   Listening, based on subject-object dichotomy, involves deliberation, discrimination, and selectivity. It is contrasted to deep
   hearing, based on nonduality.

Lotus Sutra   The Mahayana scripture that expounds the Eternal Buddha and the One Vehicle of salvation for all beings.

Mahasthāmaprāpta   Bodhisattva of wisdom who along with the bodhisattva of compassion, Avalokiteśvara, are constant companions of Amida Buddha.

Maitreya   The future Buddha who will appear in our world in 5,670,000,000 years.

Mappō   The term describing the third of the three time periods in Buddhism: Period of True Dharma (five hundred years), Period of Simulated Dharma (one thousand years), and Period of Corrupt Dharma (ten thousand years). Variations on the time divisions exist, but as far as Shinran is concerned, *mappō* is not simply historical but existential; hence the corrupted nature of reality is descriptive of the human condition, whether past, present, or future.

Myokonin   Literally means "a rare and exceptional person," generally of humble origins and with no formal education who lived the nembutsu in daily life. Myokonin are likened to the beautiful lotus flowers that bloom in muddy waters, but they are not "saints," for they are not holy nor are they canonized.

Name   Translation of *myōgō*, the ultimate reality that is Amida Buddha.

Name-that-calls   Interpretive translation of nembutsu, suggesting the central concern of great compassion for karmic beings in samsara.

Namu-amida-butsu   This is the Name of Amida Buddha that affirms each person (*namu*) embraced by great compassion (*amida-butsu*).

Nembutsu   This term that refers to namu-amida-butsu has a twofold connotation. When understood as Name or *myōgō*, it is ultimate reality; and when used for the vocalizing of the Name, it is the saying of the Name.

Nonduality   This is not a simple negation of duality, but negation of the ego-self that confronts the world. This negation affirms the multiplicity inherent in the phenomenal world from a non-egocentric position.

Non-origination of all things   The wisdom to perceive the emptiness of phenomenal reality.

Nonretrogression   The bodhisattva stage that no longer backslides or retrogresses to earlier, spiritually undeveloped stages. In Shin Buddhism it is descriptive of true entrusting that is not an act undertaken by a person but is the manifestation of Amida Buddha in one's life.

Other Power   Great compassion that defies objectification (nondualistic) but is involved in the spiritual life of all beings. According to Shinran, "Other Power is that which is free of any form of calculation." See *Letters of Shinran*, p. 39.

Parinirvāṇa   The death of the Buddha as the final act that completes his life on earth.

Path of Pure Land   The tradition within Mahayana Buddhism open to all people and teaching the ultimate transcendence of suffering through the working of great compassion.

Path of Sages   The monastic schools of Buddhism, such as Zen, which require renunciation of family life, observance of precepts, celibacy, and dietary restrictions with the goal of realizing wisdom.

Primal Vow   Although used to describe all forty-eight vows of Amida, it is primarily used as a synonym for the eighteenth vow.

Pure Land   The realm of enlightened beings, but today used most frequently to refer to the Western realm of Amida Buddha.

Self-cultivation   The physical, psychological, and spiritual discipline that aims at the embodiment of true reality.

Self-power   One's self-generated efforts to break through into liberation and freedom, yet a limited, finite being can never fully realize the goal that is infinite. According to Shinran, "Self-power is the effort to attain birth, whether by invoking the names of Buddhas other than Amida and practicing good acts other than the nembutsu, in accordance with your particular circumstances and opportunities; or by endeavoring to make yourself worthy through amending the confusion in your acts, words, and thoughts, confident of your own power and guided by your own calculations." *Letters of Shinran*, pp. 22–23.

Shinjin   Faith as true entrusting; for fuller explanation, see true entrusting.

Six Letters   This is used as a synonym for the nembutsu, based on the fact that it is written with six letters: na, mu, a, mi, da, butsu.

Sundry teachings and practices   A technical term first used by Shan-tao to cover teachings and practices other than single-hearted recitative nembutsu.

Tathāgata   Translated into East Asian languages as "One who has come from the world of suchness" (*tathā-agata*), it is used as the synonym of the Buddha. This term was also rendered as "One who has gone to the world of suchness" (*tathā-gata*) but never enjoyed wide usage.

Three Minds   The three key terms in the eighteenth vow: sincere mind, joyful entrusting, and aspiration for birth in the Pure Land. Shinran changed them from human attitudes essential for the religious life to the working of the Buddha within each of us that fulfills the religious life.

Transformation (*ten*)   The central religious experience in Shin Buddhism, whereby evil is transformed into good by the power of great compassion.

Triple Sutras   The basic Pure Land scriptures that include *The Larger Sutra of Pure Land, The Smaller Sutra of Pure Land,* and *The Sutra on Contemplating Amida Buddha.*

True entrusting (*shinjin*)   This has two connotations: 1) the *true* mind and heart of Amida Buddha infusing the foolish mind and heart of sentient beings, and 2) thereby making possible the *entrusting* of self to Amida.

Truly settled   The ultimate state of true entrusting where all doubts have vanished and perfect enlightenment is assured.

Unhindered Light   A frequent synonym for Amida, signifying the penetrating power of the Light of compassion that nothing can hinder or obstruct. It illuminates the darkness of ignorance and transforms it into the content of enlightenment.

Virtue (*toku*)   Frequently found in English translation of Pure Land works, it connotes the realization of one's fullest potential made possible by embodying the dharma (*adhigama-dharma*).

INDEX

Printed in the United States
by Baker & Taylor Publisher Services